The Doctor-Manager

Cover illustration: 'The Meeting' by John Sutherst

The Doctor-Manager

John Sutherst
Consultant Obstetrician & Gynaecologist and Clinical Director,
Arrowe Park Hospital, Wirral NHS Trust,
Merseyside

Veronica Glascott
Business Manager,
Obstetrics & Gynaecology,
Arrowe Park Hospital,
Wirral NHS Trust,
Merseyside

CHURCHILL LIVINGSTONE
EDINBURGH LONDON MADRID MELBOURNE NEW YORK AND TOKYO 1994

CHURCHILL LIVINGSTONE
Medical Division of Longman Group UK Limited

Distributed in the United States of America by Churchill Livingstone Inc., 650 Avenue of the Americas, New York, N.Y. 10011, and by associated companies, branches and representatives throughout the world.

First published 1994

ISBN 0-443-04862-2

British Library Cataloguing in Publication Data
A catalogue record for this book is available from the British Library.

Library of Congress Cataloguing in Publication Data
A catalog record for this book is available from the Library of Congress.

The publisher's policy is to use **paper manufactured from sustainable forests**

Printed in Great Britain by The Bath Press, Avon

Preface

This book has been written to help those doctors who want to become involved with management following the NHS reforms, and for all those who think that they should know something about medical management. It has not been written as a reference manual but more as a diary of how we have been affected by, and responded to, the introduction of the Clinical Directorate system.

The feature throughout is the management of change: ironically, change has caused us the greatest difficulty. During the book's gestation, NHS organisation has changed so exponentially that we have had to rewrite sections over again. For example, the description of a Business Manager (Chapter 2) bears no resemblance now to what it did a year ago: the triumvirate system of Business Manager, Clinical Nurse Manager and Clinical Director is being replaced in many Trusts by a Generic Business Manager/Clinical Director structure.

The pressures on a doctor–manager 2–3 years ago were largely internal and arose from the Resource Management Initiative (RMI). Now the pressure is to keep the business alive by responding to external pressures, e.g. changing purchaser priorities and GP fundholding. The Clinical Directorate system (upon which this book is based) is only beginning to develop in some areas and yet is already fading in others. Devolution of budgets down to small units (the ideal of RMI) is now seen to be incompatible in some Trusts with Central Management.

Examples and experiences quoted throughout the text are often drawn from our Obstetric and Gynaecology Directorate but also from anecdotal experience from colleagues around the country. They have been chosen to be easily translated by other specialties.

Clearly, the NHS is in a period of immense change and the answers to certain problems are not yet understood. Exercises in collaboration between what were previously described as management and medicine must be encouraged. This is how this book started.

Chapter 1 briefly describes the history of the NHS and its recent reforms. The implication of these for doctors, namely the expectation that they be more involved with management, is amplified later in the book.

In Chapter 2 the Clinical Director model is described. Arrowe Park was one of the original RMI sites and so Clinical Directorates began to be developed here in 1986/1987. In other hospitals they only started after Trust status in 1991. Therefore, throughout the text there will be reference to the Clinical Director, although this is meant to indicate doctor–manager in a broader sense. In Chapter 2 we also describe the management structure within which we work: this will vary from one

Directorate/hospital to another, so a certain degree of interpretation may be necessary when the descriptions are applied to other departments. Chapters 3–6 are probably applicable to most units, with some modification. There were some differences of opinion between us regarding the amount and quality of management detail needed in this book. Whilst it is probably one of the few books written by a doctor and manager together and, as such, should contain equal contributions from both sources, its readership is aimed at doctors moving into management. Therefore, we have concentrated on the practical aspects of this step rather than the theoretical aspects of business management. If any deficiencies in the book are seen to arise because of this, they are due to the insistance by one of us (JRS) that some business detail be omitted. Nevertheless, we appreciate the importance of business theory and of the need for doctors to adopt a different stance in relation to business methods than they have done in the past, particularly when the introductory lessons have been learned. At the end of each chapter we refer the reader to larger texts for further reading.

There have also been very definite differences in opinion between us with regard to certain issues. At times we were tempted to provide the reader with each view (i.e. the problem as perceived by the Business Manager and the problem as perceived by the doctor–manager). This would have negated the main purpose of the book which is to show that managers and doctors can co-exist and present a joint solution to a problem. Some of the solutions provided are undoubtedly and unavoidably a compromise: this is the way it has to be. On other occasions we have inclined towards a medical standpoint, because the book is intended for doctor–managers.

Throughout the book we have tried to demonstrate the benefits of the new system: in Chapter 7 we highlight some anxieties about its future success. For example, in spite of impeccable attention to budgetary control in our own Directorate, and in spite of working (with difficulty) inside an agreed (albeit underfunded) budget, we find that the goalposts keep changing. This is a fact of life and part of learning how to do it. This is the management of change and changes happen all the time. This is what the book is all about.

Liverpool, 1994

JRS
VG

Contents

Acknowledgements

We wish to thank: The Consultants in other parts of the country who have kindly provided us with examples and anecdotes from their experiences in the Clinical Directorate system; The Photographic Department at Arrowe Park Hospital for the illustrations; and most of all, Madeleine and Frank, for their constructive criticism, tolerance and support during the long hours of the book's preparation.

List of abbreviations

BM	Business Manager
BMA	British Medical Association
CD	Clinical Director
CE	Chief Executive
CHC	Community Health Council
CISP	Community Information Systems Project
CMDS	Contract Minimum Data Set
CMO	Chief Medical Officer
DGH	District General Hospital
DGM	District General Manager
DHA	District Health Authority
DoH	Department of Health
DHSS	Former Department of Health & Social Security
DISP	Developing Information Systems for Purchaser
DISS	District Information Support Systems
DMC	District Medical Committee
DMU	Directly Managed Unit
DMT	District Management Team or Directorate Management Team
DRG	Diagnostic Related Group
ECR	Extra-Contractual Referral
EFL	External Financing Limit
FCE	Finished Consultant Episode
FHS	Family Health Services (formerly FPS)
FHSA	Family Health Services Authority (formerly FPC)
FPC	Family Practitioner Committee (now FHSA)
GMC	General Medical Council
GP	General practitioner
HA	Health authority
HAA	Hospital Activity Analysis
HCA	Health Care Assistant
HCHS	Hospital and Community Health Services
HIPE	Hospital Inpatient Enquiry

HISS	Hospital Information Support System
HRG	Healthcare Related Group/Health Resource Group
HSI	Health Service Indicator
IGS	Income Generation Scheme
IHSM	Institute of Health Services Management
IMGME	Information Management Group of the NHS Management Executive
IM&T	Information Management and Technology
IPR	Individual Performance Review
IS	Information Systems
IT	Information Technology
JPAC	Joint Planning Advisory Committee
LMC	Local Medical Committee
MAC	Medical Advisory Committee
MDS	Minimum Data Set
MDU	Medical Defence Union
MEO	Management Executive Outposts
MPS	Medical Protection Society
NAHAT	National Association of Health Authorities and Trusts
NHSME	National Health Service Management Executive
NM	Nurse or Clinical Nurse Manager
PAS	Patient Administration System
PCIS	Patient Centred Information System
PI	Performance Indicator
PRP	Performance Related Pay
QA	Quality Assurance
QALY	Quality Adjusted Life Year
RAWP	Resource Allocation Working Party
RCN	Royal College of Nursing
RCOG	Royal College of Obstetricians and Gynaecologists
RGM	Regional General Manager
RHA	Regional Health Authority
RMI	Resource Management Initiative
SHO	Senior house officer
SIFT	Service Increment for Teaching (now SIFTR)
SIFTR	Service Increment for Teaching and Research
SR	Senior Registrar
TQM	Total Quality Management
UDI	Unilateral Declaration of Independence

UGM	Unit General Manager
UKCC	United Kingdom Central Council for Nursing, Midwifery and Health Visiting
UMT	Unit of Medical Time (doctors in training)
VTS	Vocational Training Scheme
WTE	Whole Time Equivalent

Glossary

Bed occupancy

The number of beds occupied by patients at a particular time, usually midnight. It may be expressed as a percentage of available beds. For units that do not operate a hot-bed policy, midnight is not the best time for it to be measured.

Budget

A statement of the financial resources made available to a budget holder to provide an agreed level of service over a set period of time.

Business plan

A plan setting out the goals of an organisation and identifying the resources and actions needed to achieve them.

Cash limit

A limit imposed by the Government on the amount of cash which a Health Authority or FHSA may spend during a given financial year. Separate cash limits are set for revenue and capital.

Clinical budgeting

The allocation of specific budgets to consultant clinical staff which they are responsible for managing.

Clinical Directorate

A unit of management for specific clinical services. A Clinical Directorate is usually led by a Clinical Director, who is often a Consultant working in that role for a number of sessions per week. He/She is supported by a Business and/or Nurse (Clinical) Manager. The extent to which management responsibilities for budgets and staff are devolved to Directorates varies between hospitals.

Cold admission

Patient admitted from a waiting list.

Contracts

The basis for agreement for what services should be provided to patients.

Cost-benefit analysis

Setting the cost of particular activities against the total benefits, financial and non-financial.

Cost improvement programme

Projects designed to improve efficiency but also to cut costs and expand the service. The Government sets annual cost improvement targets. Savings from the programmes may be kept and reinvested in other services.

Cross-boundary flow

The movement of patients across administrative boundaries for treatment.

Day cases

Patients who occupy a bed for investigation or treatment who are admitted and discharged on the same day.

Day case unit

A unit used exclusively for day cases.

External financing limit

A cash limit set by the Department of Health on net external financing for an NHS Trust. A positive EFL is set where the agreed capital spending for an NHS Trust exceeds income from internally generated resources. A zero EFL is set where the agreed capital spending programme for a Trust equals internally generated resources. A negative external financing limit is set where the agreed capital spending programme for a Trust is less than internally generated resources.

Extra-contractual referrals

Referral of a patient to a provider unit which has not formally negotiated a contract with the DHA of residence of the patient.

GP fundholder

Practice with a budget which includes purchase of a range of in- and outpatient services from a provider unit.

International Classification of Diseases

Statistical classification of diseases and injuries produced by the World Health Organization.

Indicative amount

The amount allocated to GPs by the FHSA for anticipated expenditure on prescribing during a financial year.

Korner data

NHS information required by the NHS/DHSS steering group on health services information chaired by Edith Korner. The group recommended a minimum set of data which should be collected in all districts for management purposes.

Management budgeting

Annually agreed budgets are based on anticipated workload and the resources needed to meet it. Authorities' resources are allocated to budget holders for specific activities.

Virement

The authorised transference of funds from one budgetary heading to another.

1 History of the NHS and recent reforms

Introduction

The NHS has undergone a series of radical and major reforms since its inception in 1948, the 1990 National Health Service and Community Care Act being the most recent and fundamental (Table 1.1). The

Table 1.1 Major changes in the NHS since its inception

1948	NHS created. Amalgamation of Poor Law Buildings, Voluntary and Teaching Hospitals. Service was poorly costed out and expenditure was open-ended.
1962–1982	Series of Reforms included: • DGH concept • Salmon • Cogwheel • Unification of NHS • Introduction of Cash Limits • RAWP • 'Patients First' reorganisation—abolished multi-district Area Health Authorities in an attempt to devolve decision making nearer to the operational level. The general feeling was there were too many administrative tiers.
1983	Griffiths. Introduced new general management system. Clinicians in Management. Start of Resource Management Initiative and Clinical Directorates.
1986	Resource Management Initiative.
1989	'Working for Patients' and 'Caring for People' White Papers.
1990	National Health Service and Community Care Act. Purchaser/provider separation; NHS Trusts; GP Fundholding.
1993	Langlands' Review.

changes may be seen as predictable, as politicians have striven to control the huge bureaucratic organisation which employs over a million people, consumes almost 5.5% of the Gross Domestic Product (1992/1993) and which affects the lives of the entire electorate. By legislation, not only the structure, but also the very basis of the NHS has been transformed.

Doctors at all levels are now expected to be increasingly involved in decisions about planning, organisation and management of the NHS. The purpose of this chapter is to provide the context within which management changes have occurred and to explain how doctors have become more involved.

Historical perspective

Between 1962 and 1982 there were a series of reforms and during this period the NHS was 'administered' rather than 'managed'. Figure 1.1 shows how the service was split.

A major reform was implemented in 1974 when an attempt was made to unify the NHS (Fig. 1.2): teaching hospitals lost their separate status; Area Health Authorities (AHAs) were created with District Management Teams (DMTs) under them to plan a united service around the new District General Hospitals (DGHs). But GPs, hospital consultants, nurses, adminstrators and treasurers had an equal voice (and veto) on the DMTs, so management was only possible by consensus. This reorganisation did reduce the number of authorities but failed to secure full unification. Furthermore, plans to redistribute resources in order to even out previous disparities and devote more to deprived groups and areas came to grief because of the financial crises at the time (the start of a recession in 1973 and the sudden rise in oil prices). The Treasury had to introduce cash limits on public expenditure (1976). Later came compulsory competitive tendering and year-on-year cost improvement programmes (1984).

In 1982 an attempt was made to salvage the reforms via the 'Patients First' Health Service reorganisation in which 90 AHAs were replaced by 200 District Health Authorities (DHAs), which had greater freedom to plan. However, as the pressure on the service to live within allocated resources grew, the consensus management approach was increasingly criticised, and in 1983 the Government set up the NHS Management Enquiry under Sir Roy Griffiths of Sainsburys.

The introduction of general management following Griffiths' 1983 report has had far-reaching implications for the NHS. The report highlighted the absence of identifiable leaders within NHS management. It was difficult to see who was in charge in a particular locality. Griffiths recommended the introduction of general managers at Regional, District and Hospital level and an end to the 'consensus' approach to decision making.

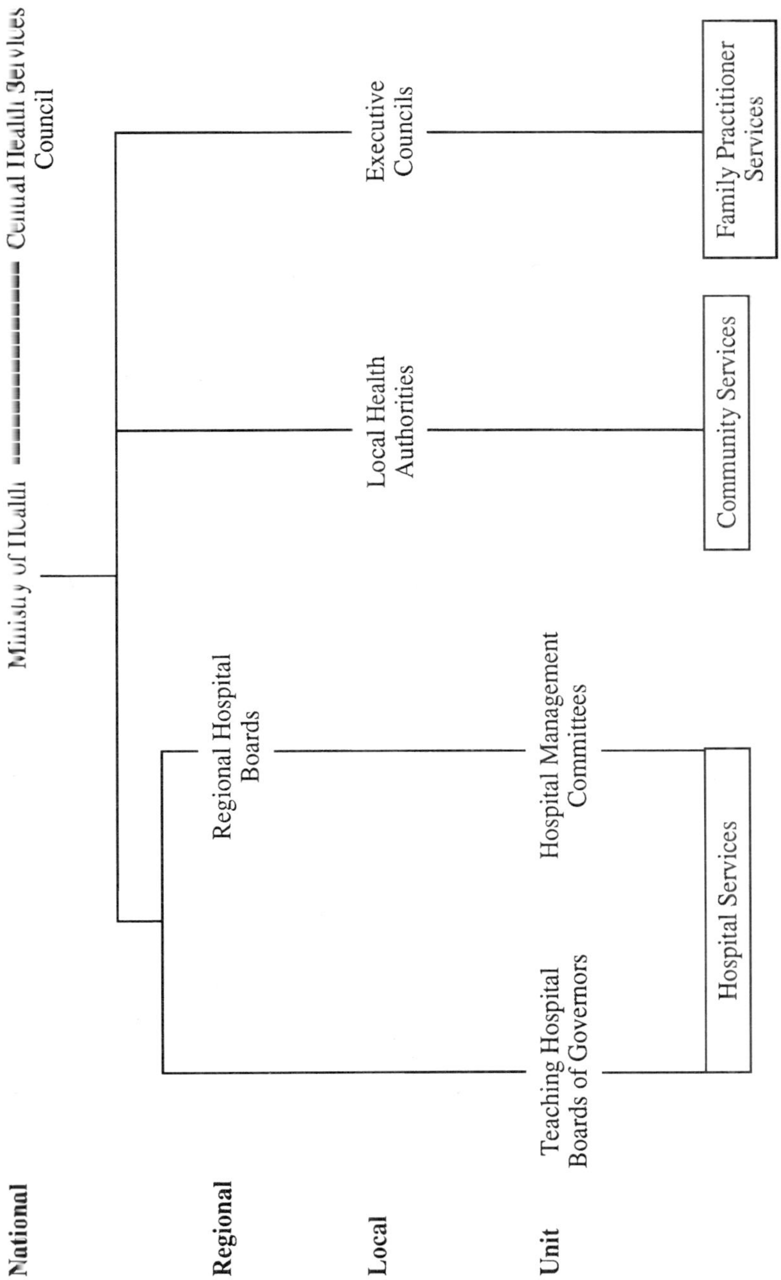

Figure 1.1 The NHS 1948–74 (Reproduced with permission from Ham & Merry 1993)

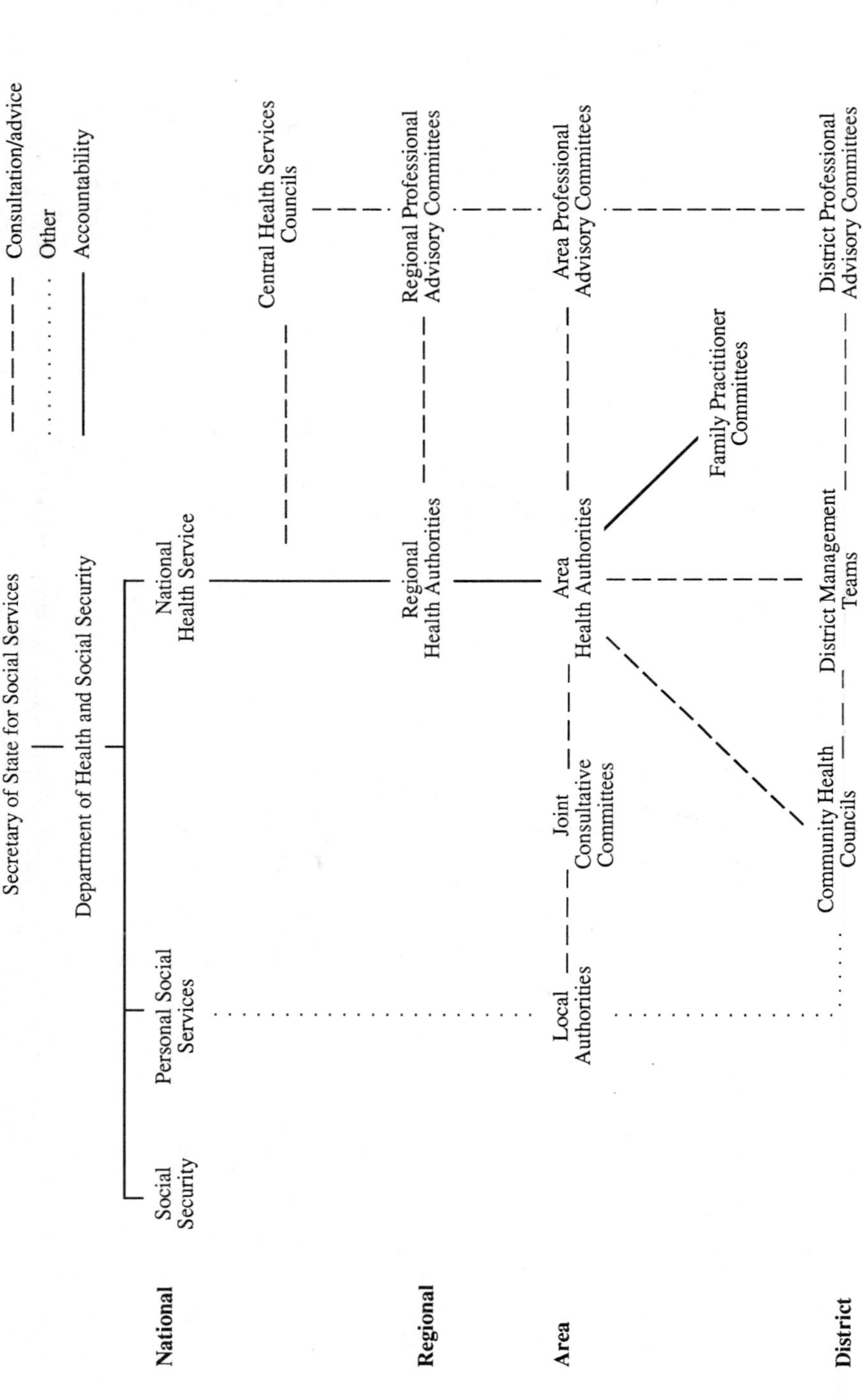

Figure 1.2 The reorganised NHS in 1974 (Reproduced with permission from Ham & Merry 1993)

The most recent reforms (from 1989) not only require doctors to play a central role in health service management but they also change the structure and financial organisation of the NHS. Throughout the recent period of change, the Government has resisted any argument that the NHS is underfunded, preferring to insist that every opportunity be explored by NHS managers and doctors to make the best use of the resources available. So, to gain maximum benefit for their patients and clinical practice from these new conditions, it is necessary for doctors to have an appreciation of the philosophy behind the changes as well as an understanding of their practical effects.

Management changes

Resource management

The White Paper (Working for Patients 1989) reiterated Griffiths' recommendations that clinicians be encouraged to become more involved through resource management. The emphasis was to involve medical and nursing staff much more centrally in the budgetary process. In 1986 six hospitals became pilot sites for the Resource Management Initiative (RMI) (Arrowe Park Hospital, Wirral; Freeman Hospital, Newcastle; Guy's, Lewisham and North Southwark, London; Royal Infirmary, Huddersfield; Pilgrim Hospital, Lincolnshire; Royal Hampshire Hospital, Winchester). Because of this early involvement, the clinicians at these hospitals have had several years' experience of management budgeting (albeit limited) via a Clinical Directorate system.

The aim of RMI was to plan, deliver and cost patient care more effectively (Fig. 1.3). The three most important components of the project involved:

- developing a credible clinical database (reflecting accurate diagnostic and operational coding);
- establishing a case-mix management system for recording patient treatment resource usage and costs;
- implementing effective nurse management systems.

Medical audit

Resource management also emphasised the importance of the development of measures of outcome of service provision. One of the key

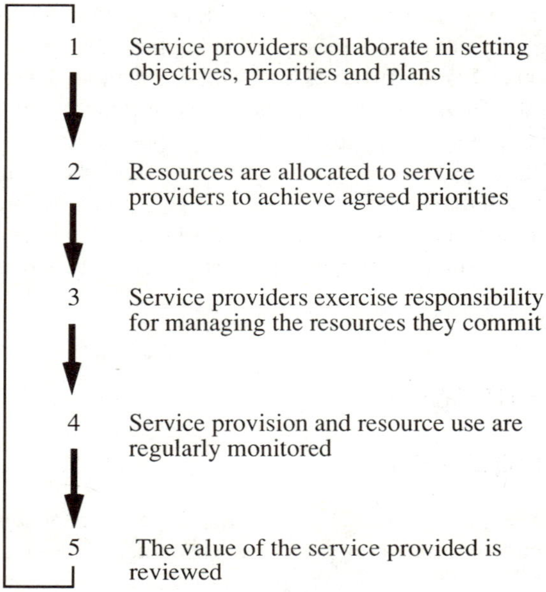

Figure 1.3 The resource management process
(Reproduced with permission from Buxton et al 1991)

features of the NHS reforms was the requirement for doctors to carry out medical audit. The White Paper required that each health district should have in place a system of medical audit by 1991, and should give directions for the establishment of audit committees.

The White Paper defined medical audit as:

'The systematic, critical analysis of the quality of medical care, including procedures used for diagnosis and treatment, the use of resources and the resulting outcome and quality of life for the patient'.

(Working for Patients 1989)

The Royal Colleges added more purpose to this definition by emphasising that audit is an effective educational tool (Royal College of Physicians 1989, Royal College of Surgeons of London 1989).

Medical audit is discussed in greater detail in Chapter 4.

Consumer focus

The political drive for change was underpinned by a desire to create a more consumer-orientated service, to allow finance to follow patients to the more efficient hospitals and units, and to raise the importance of the measurement of clinical outcomes into the management arena.

Separation of funding and provision

The essential feature of the new NHS structure is the separation of the provision of health care from that of its financing. Hence the introduction of the terms 'internal market', 'purchaser', 'provider' and the 'contract' into the NHS vocabulary. The previous system whereby hospitals were accountable to, and financed by, DHAs – who were in turn accountable to Regional Health Authorities (RHAs) and from there on up to the Department of Health, has been revised to allow an 'internal market' to develop and regulate the provision of health care. All services to patients are now provided through the means of a contract between hospitals (as providers of the services) and Health Authorities or GP fundholders (as purchasers, providing the cash).

Resource allocation

The distribution of NHS revenue is in two directions: to the Hospital and Community Health Service (HCHS) and to the Family Health Service (FHS) (Fig. 1.4). The former covers DHAs and the latter contracted services such as GPs, dentists, opticians and pharmacists. One of the recommendations of the Langlands' Review (1993, see p. 12) is the 'active encouragement' of mergers between DHAs and FHSAs, and legislation is expected to enable such mergers. In addition, GP fundholders are now allocated their own budgets to buy secondary care for their patients.

Part of the NHS budget is top-sliced to fund special initiatives and services (e.g. the earmarking of money for *waiting list initiatives*).

Purchasers

Regional Health Authorities

Whilst RHAs retain overall strategic responsibility for planning, resource allocation and monitoring of health provision and the performance of the Districts, they also assume the responsibility for managing Family Health Service Authorities (FHSAs, formerly Family Practitioner Committees) – thereby drawing the GPs into the management processes at Regional level.

The role RHAs had in providing advice and assistance to Trusts,

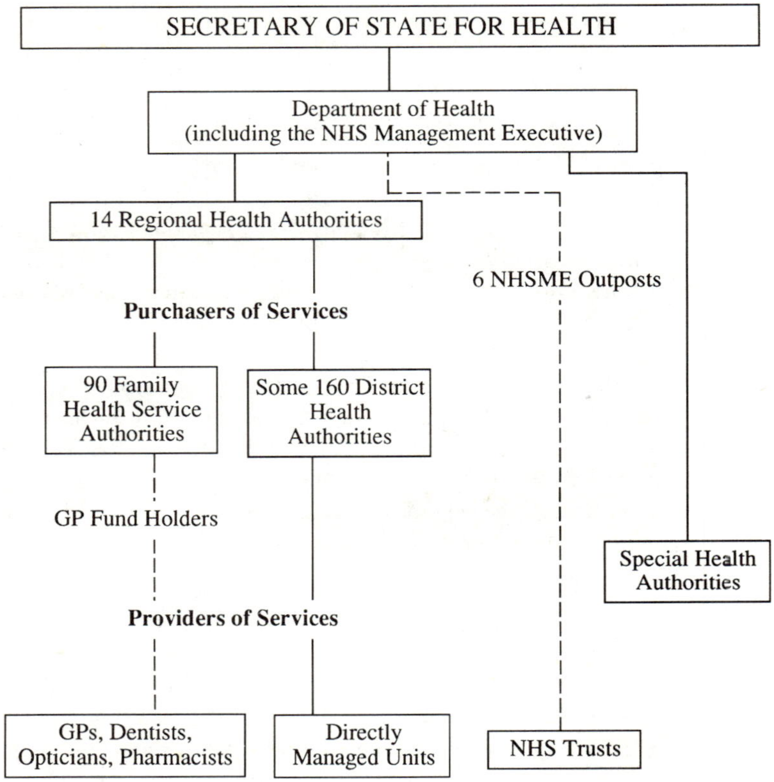

Figure 1.4 Organisation of the NHS in England, 1993 (Reproduced with permission from Ham & Merry 1993)

overseeing new funding systems and contract developments, monitoring the relationship between purchaser and provider and ensuring there is no distortion of priorities in service provision, is now being taken over by Trust Outposts (see p. 11). However, if purchaser and provider cannot agree, RHAs have an arbitration role.

Following the Langlands' Review (see p. 12), legislation will be introduced in the 1994–95 parliamentary session to abolish the 14 Regions and replace them and the existing Management Executive Outposts, with eight new regional offices; this will take effect from 1 April 1996.

District Health Authorities

Prior to the 1990 Act, all hospitals were managed by DHAs. Now 292 (April 1993) hospitals have become NHS Trusts and are free of

District management control. Others have remained under the control of the DHA as Directly Managed Units (DMUs), but it is likely that a further 100–140 will become Trusts in April 1994 (99 are already approved).

In the short term, Districts have to combine their purchasing responsibilities with those of managing hospitals which are not NHS Trusts. This is an apparent conflict of interest, although it is unlikely to exist for long as more hospitals apply for Trust status. This will allow DHAs to focus their attention on purchasing functions, i.e. to:

- assess local health needs;
- draw up service contracts;
- negotiate with providers;
- monitor contract performance.

In some areas, notably London and the larger conurbations, Districts have formed purchasing consortia to negotiate service contracts on their behalf. However, the statutory responsibility for determining the health needs of the population remains with the District.

Each DHA has the responsibility to ensure that within available resources, services are secured to meet the health needs of its resident population. Districts are free to purchase health care from any hospital which can meet the service specifications, including units in the private and voluntary sectors.

Family Health Services Authorities

The 1990 Act changed the name of Family Practitioner Committees to Family Health Services Authorities and placed them in a direct management relationship with RHAs. FHSAs are responsible for purchasing and managing the services provided by GPs. They negotiate the terms and conditions of service under which GPs work in the NHS. Their role is being strengthened to include more financial involvement with GP practice developments. They will be able to target resources where they are most needed. FHSAs will be taking the lead in conjunction with DHAs in assessing the health needs of the population and commissioning primary care services to meet those needs. FHSAs and DHAs are still *statutorily* separate entities, but following the Langlands' Review (p. 12) legislation is expected to enable DHA/FHSA mergers. In some areas there already exists a combined management arrangement. It is envisaged that they will become a combined purchasing organisation under statute across primary and secondary fields of care.

An important function of FHSA work is to liaise with the RHA on the introduction of GP fundholding practices. Each RHA includes an FHSA chairman amongst its membership.

Fundholding practices

The 1990 Act made it possible for any general practitioner to apply to the relevant RHA for recognition as a 'fundholding practice'. The conditions for applicants are laid down by the Secretary of State. Originally it was thought that only practices with over 11 000 registered patients would be eligible, but this limit has been reduced. The Government is now encouraging smaller practices to apply. There are now 1120 GP fundholders (since April 1993); 600 more are expected by 1st April 1994.

RHAs are required to allocate money (from the allocation of the relevant DHA) to participating GPs, who are then able to use the money to purchase elective procedures in acute hospitals and (from April 1993) Community Services relating to the function of District Nurses and Health Visitors.

Other areas of purchasing available to fundholders are:

- outpatient services;
- X-rays and laboratory tests;
- certain inpatient and day-case treatments;
- drugs (the budget for drugs prescribed has given GPs the incentive to examine their prescribing and referral patterns);
- employment of practice staff.

Fundholding practices are monitored by the FHSA which holds the allocated money and pays the bills. The Government's aim is to move to a fundholding formula in which the money fundholders receive is based on the number of patients served, adjusted for age, sex, etc. This will replace the current funding formula, which allocates resources according to the past use of services and the hospital referral patterns of GPs.

Non-fundholding GPs will be expected to keep their yearly expenditure within an 'indicative amount' for drugs and appliances (set by the FHSA), and are encouraged to refer patients to hospitals with which the DHA has contracts — apart from exceptional cases which become *extra contractual referrals*.

Providers

NHS Trusts

NHS Trusts are self-governing units providing hospital and community services within the NHS and were first established in 1991 under the NHS reforms. They are run by boards of directors and are accountable directly to the Secretary of State without any intervention from RHAs and DHAs (but their performance is monitored by Management Executive Outposts, see below). They are free to:

- develop their own management structures;
- employ their own staff;
- set terms and conditions of service themselves (except for junior doctors);
- acquire and sell assets;
- borrow money (subject to annual limits).

Each Trust must prepare an annual business plan and publish an annual report and accounts. Trusts receive their income from contracts with DHAs and GP fundholders and are responsible to those purchasers for delivering the quantity and quality of care in specified contracts. They are statutorily required to break even and to achieve such financial objectives as may be set by the Secretary of State.

It is in the first- and second-wave Trusts that the most effort and innovation is evident in terms of developing management and information systems that require the full involvement of doctors. This has probably happened because Trust status was at first only awarded to those hospitals (57 in the first wave) with doctors well established in management programmes. Hospitals which had been involved with the RMI as pilot units clearly fell in this category and because of RM were already experienced in management budgeting by doctors. This group of hospitals has thus far demonstrated the most expertise in 'doctor–management.'

Outposts

The performance of NHS Trusts is monitored by six Outposts of the Management Executive. These review the business plans of the Trusts and assess performance against plans. A wide-ranging investigation and review of the arrangements and responsibilities relating to NHS management above the level of local health care purchasers and providers (the intermediate tier) was announced by the Secretary of State in February 1993. This review was set up as The Langlands' Review (Alan Langlands is now the Chief Executive of the NHSME) and was chaired by management consultant Kate Jenkins. The terms of reference of the review team were, briefly, to carry out an organisational analysis of the main work and functions required to:

- ensure NHS 1991 reforms are fully effective;
- ensure effective oversight of purchasers and providers;
- ensure the proportion of expenditure relating to direct patient care is maximised.

The recommendations were expected to determine the statutory responsibilities and core functions discharged by bodies directly accountable to central Government and to determine the organisational structure these require. In addition, the review was asked to consider changes in the configuration of NHS purchasers, e.g. DHA mergers, DHA/FHSA joint working and the development of the GP fundholding scheme.

The Review reported in November 1993 and recommends the replacement of the 14 RHAs and 6 Management Executive Outposts with a single tier of 8 regional offices. Where possible, existing Outpost and RHA boundaries will be maintained. These regional offices will be responsible for the development of purchasing and for monitoring Trusts. Legislation to enable this restructuring is expected in the 1994–95 parliamentary session and will take effect from 1 April 1996.

At purchaser level, the Review recommends the merger of DHAs and FHSAs to establish one authority at local level and to integrate purchasing across primary and secondary care boundaries.

Directly Managed Units

These also have to compete for contracts in the internal market. They have greater freedom than before to run their own affairs, and must produce business plans, but have none of the specific powers accorded to Trusts. The DMU is monitored and managed by the DHA, which creates an inherent tension as the DHA is also the main purchaser, but increasingly a distance is developing as Districts devolve their staff to hospital level and begin to concentrate on their purchaser role. It is envisaged that a total separation of DMUs from the DHA will be the way forward, and that NHS Trust status will become the model of choice for provider units. The first wave was established in April 1991, the second in April 1992.

The third wave in 1993 means that 292 units are now NHS Trusts and together employ 85% of all NHS staff. It is likely that all DMUs will eventually become Trusts.

Nature of the contract

Contracts are the means through which health authorities and provider units agree on the required quality, quantity and cost of the services secured for the population. Purchasers have the freedom and opportunity to place contracts wherever they feel the best value is to be obtained — whether in terms of quality of care, convenience for patients or value for money. *This effectively leaves hospitals without a guaranteed income: the funds they receive are entirely dependent upon the contracts placed with them.*

In negotiating contracts, the purchasers strive to improve features of service delivery, the most notable example being the reduction of waiting times for hospital admission. Another thrust is a shift in the balance of services provided from secondary to primary care.

In assessing the health requirements of its resident population the DHA has to distinguish between 'core' services — those for which patients need guaranteed access (mainly emergency services), and 'non-core' services (typically planned non-emergency surgery).

There are currently three types of contract:

- *Block contracts*, in which the provider is paid an annual sum in instalments, in return for access by the purchaser's patients to a defined range of services with an agreed level of activity. Emergency services fall into this category.
- *Cost and Volume contracts*, in which the provider receives a sum in return for treating a specified number of patients. These are applicable to large volumes of planned surgery (e.g. varicose veins, hysterectomy, tonsillectomy).
- *Cost per Case contracts*, in which the purchaser agrees the price to be paid for the treatment of individual patients. These are initially applicable to specialist treatments, but some specific conditions and operative procedures are currently dealt with under this type of contract.

The NHSME is pressing for all contracts to be cost and volume and cost per case by 1995, phasing out the block contract, although it remains to be seen whether information/case-mix and financial systems will allow this shift to develop effectively.

A small number of patient referrals are not predictable and hence cannot be covered by contracts. They are known as extra contractual referrals (ECRs) and may require emergency or non-emergency treatment. The purchaser in the area of residence of the patient is required to pay for the emergency treatment, but for the non-emergency cases, the provider is obliged to obtain approval from the purchaser before treatment commences.

All purchasers, Districts, FHSAs and GP fundholders, have specified quality dimensions to the contracts struck with provider units. Whilst the technicalities of the contracting process may be dealt with by a management finance and marketing team within a hospital, the agreeing of quality targets and performance indicators requires the *full* involvement of clinicians. In many instances clinicians are still distanced from the process of contracting. If you are interested in getting into the management arena, a fundamental step is involvement in the contracting process. Without this the contract is liable to fail. It is recognised nationally that doctors are essential to this process, and increasingly you will be expected to have more detailed discussion/review/involvement at a clinical level with purchasers (e.g. with Directors and Consultants in Public Health).

The guidance to Districts as purchasers from the Department of Health stresses the key role to be played by GPs in the contracting process. The decision of GPs on where to refer patients has a major influence on the use of hospital services. Equally, their views on the quality of service will determine areas where service improvements are required. Developing the dialogue with GPs is one of the fundamental requirements for securing the future of hospital services. The clinical relationship between consultant and GP has to be a priority for consultants in management.

Impact of reforms on hospitals and staff

GP fundholding

The advent of GP fundholders is perhaps the most radical change in the NHS since its inception. GP practices that have joined the fundholding process generally each have in excess of 7000 patients registered with them. The number of referrals from such large practices can be high and so securing contracts with them can mean substantial income for the provider unit. It follows that the reverse is true if the business goes elsewhere.

It is anticipated that by 1994 most, if not all, NHS services will be provided by NHS Trusts. More than 75% of the population will be registered with fundholding practices, so there will be an almost complete separation of purchaser and provider roles.

Hospital practice will depend on securing contracts. As 75% of a hospital's revenue budget is devoted to salaries, loss of income due to the inability to secure contracts will mean loss of jobs.

Also, hospitals will have to learn to move quickly in order to meet the requirements of the purchasers. GPs are very keen to become true partners in the care of patients and so may have no hesitation in moving patients to units where their requirements are met. These shifts in referral patterns might happen overnight...they are not issues upon which hospital staff can deliberate for months. Hospitals will have to learn how to organise their workforces more flexibly — appropriate skill-mix of staff; job-sharing programmes; locum, temporary and part-time staff — as the need demands. They will have to be able to expand or contract their workforce at short notice. They will have to observe and study market forces more closely than ever before. This will be difficult because this sort of flexibility is not prevalent inside institutions like hospitals.

GPs, as opposed to larger purchasers (e.g. DHAs), have more flexibility because of the relatively small number of patients in their charge, and so do not threaten the viability of hospitals, but in the future there is likely to be an amalgamation of purchaser power which will be able to do so.

GPs are also developing services within their own surgeries, e.g. the provision for minor surgical and diagnostic procedures, and are insisting that 'peripheral clinics' be conducted on their premises by senior hospital medical staff so that patients can attend and be followed-up more easily. If cooperation between GP and hospital doctor is the essence of this type of deal it will probably enhance patient care dramatically, although some hospital doctors doubt the motives and cost-effectiveness of such moves. A compromise might be the development of 'locality clinics' where a section of the District's population (registered with a group of GPs) can be seen by visiting consultants.

The objective behind the purchaser/provider split is that patients should get a better deal. By injecting more competition into the system via the internal market, it is expected that funding will follow patients to the more efficient provider units. However, the purchaser will make judgements based on outcomes (which should really be the yardstick) as well as price. As yet outcomes are not measured properly and hospitals are finding difficulty in implementing meaningful audit of outcome programmes.

Clearly, the perception of what services a hospital should provide will differ between clinicians, particularly between those in the community (who will argue that a primary care viewpoint is the most valid) and those in hospital (who may argue that a specialist view is more valid).

Medical views are always going to differ and so it is important that patients' needs are not compromised and that all medical views are heard where they matter, i.e. in the purchasing arenas. The fear amongst hospital doctors is that patients may only be allowed a one-sided view of treatment options. The development of partnerships between GP, hospital doctor and DPH is crucial if prejudicial management is to be avoided.

Rationing

The radical nature of the NHS reforms has exposed the concept of care rationing to public debate. Health care has always been the subject of rationing, with access restricted or controlled by queuing or GPs acting as 'gate keepers'. Until recently, however, rationing was *implicit* rather than *explicit* and bound up with clinical judgements about whether treatment was appropriate or not.

In the new 'market' climate of the NHS, there is pressure to contain costs and generally to do more with less. The purchaser/provider split demands that purchasers place contracts for explicit services, and in the process, they have to be precise about what is bought in terms of quantity and quality, and conversely, what they are not prepared to buy. The choices are no longer to be left to doctors alone. However, doctors as managers are central in the search for a better way of deciding health care allocation priorities. It is important that you understand and take on board the other key element of the reforms, which is the emphasis on '*consumerism*'. Consulting the public and pressure groups on health care provision, down to the level of locality purchasing, is leading to a shift from professionally-led health services, to services that reflect public preferences and perceived local health needs.

Whilst assessment of local health needs and provision of hospital and community capacity to match those needs is technically the responsibility of the purchasers, it is essential that the service you provide is responsible to locally articulated views and is able to adapt to changing priorities.

Example.

An Orthopaedics Directorate felt 'under-resourced' in terms of its capacity to meet public demand for its services. The conclusions of a review which encompassed primary, community and acute care, were radically to reorganise the investment in and access to the physiotherapy service, to streamline subspecialist clinical service and to enforce jointly agreed GP referral and follow-up protocols.

This had the effect of reducing inappropriate referrals to the waiting lists, allowing direct access to physiotherapy for certain conditions and releasing resource for use in ways agreed jointly by professionals in hospital, GPs and their patients. It also satisfied a purchaser priority of shifting the emphasis of service provision from the acute to the primary sector.

There may be a temptation for doctor–managers or managers to turn to techniques such as QALYS or the Oregon experiment for structure or guidance in the messy search to make sense of explicit rationing (see p. 171). It is important to recognise that these do not provide a simple solution to complex problems.

Consumer participation

In recent years there has been a marked development in formalising the patient's role as partner in the care provided in the hospital or community setting. The agreement of treatment/care plans is central to this process, and on a broader front most units/departments will conduct patient satisfaction exercises to determine consumer response to the overall service given at the time of treatment.

Purchasers will require evidence of consumer satisfaction levels in their contractual agreements with the provider unit, and it is in the interest of all members of the specialty that this is used to shape and develop service delivery.

In the longer term, purchasers will use the priorities of localities to determine the nature, quantity and quality of services provided. Far-sighted clinicians will seek to participate in this process.

Summary

There have been immense changes in the NHS during the last few years, beginning with the Griffiths Report in 1983 and continuing through to the present and undoubtedly into the future. They have been made even more dramatic by the scale of the operations: the NHS is a huge service industry, employing over a million people and spending over £34 billion on providing health care for 58 million people (1992–93).

The most fundamental of these changes have been:

- the increasing expectation for doctors to become involved with management;

- the split between purchaser and provider with the generation of an internal market;
- the advent of GP fundholding;
- the shift in emphasis from secondary to primary health care.

The speed of change and its magnitude are having far reaching effects on staff in the NHS, as is discussed in the following chapters.

Further reading

Buxton M, Packwood T, Keen J
1991 Final Report of the Brunel University Evaluation of Resource Management. Health Economics Research Group, DoH. HMSO, London

Connah B, Pearson R (eds)
1990 NAHAT 1990 NHS Handbook, 7th edn. The MacMillan Press , London

Griffiths R
1983 NHS Management Enquiry (The Griffiths Report). DHSS. HMSO, London

Ham C
1991 The New National Health Service, Organisation and Management. Radcliffe Medical Press, Oxford

Ham C, Merry P (eds)
1993 NAHAT NHS Handbook, 8th edn. JMH Publishing, Tunbridge Wells, Kent

Health of the Nation
1992. HMSO, London

National Health Service and Community Care Act
1990. HMSO, London

Royal College of Physicians of London
1989 Medical audit: a first report. Royal College of Physicians, London

Royal College of Surgeons of London
1989 Guidelines to clinical audit in surgical practice. Royal College of Surgeons, London

Working for Patients
1989 Working Papers Nos. 1–9. HMSO, London

2 The clinician in management

Introduction

Background and undergraduate training

Griffiths argued that doctors should adopt a managerial role because they are the ones who spend NHS money and therefore they should be accountable for its use. From this arose the concept of resource management and from there came the idea of encouraging one doctor — the Clinical Director — to represent a group of doctors from one specialty (or from a small number of related specialties) and to act as their advocate in managing a part of the hospital's resource as effectively and as efficiently as possible.

However, for some people medicine and management start from such different points they cannot be mixed. A survey of 55 District General Managers (Scrivens 1988a) showed that the non-medically qualified ones had grave doubts about doctors' abilities to become managers. They did not see medical training as being relevant for management and several thought that doctors would not cope with the tensions of management. They argued that budget-holding doctors might not take seriously the need to keep within budget — after all, a consultant overspending his/her budget is unlikely to be sacked.

Many doctors would acquiesce with this view. They are already extremely busy; they probably have had no formal training in management; and many regard financial management skills as being irrelevant to their careers. Furthermore, the undergraduate training they have had is to provide the best possible care for their patients regardless of cost. Extensive and expensive investigations are encouraged in order to make a diagnosis. There is an often-quoted joke which describes a 'normal' person as one who has not been investigated enough!

If this were not enough, senior doctors have seen a number of management changes each of which has prophesied better patient care if there was greater doctor involvement, but each has been discarded in favour of yet another system. However, the present NHS reforms are more fundamental than any that have gone before in the history of the NHS and cannot be ignored.

There can be no question of the present-day consultant absolving him or herself of some managerial duty — however small this may be. The minimum requirement may be simply to agree that a colleague takes the lead and that you work as part of the team.

If you are the one with sufficient drive to take the lead, you should use the communication, teaching and counselling skills you have acquired during your medical training to develop your managerial skills. It should be stressed that these medical skills need to be packaged and applied differently to be valuable in management. One cannot extrapolate from the one-to-one interpersonal skills which you have learned so far to those needed to motivate a workforce. Those skills have to be deployed in different ways to different staff groups.

Management courses

Since the Griffiths report, management courses for clinicians have emerged. As yet it is not clear which courses are valuable and which ones not. There is a plethora of them — some of them taking up so much of a clinician's time that one wonders how they can be cost-effective. Indeed, one can ask should doctors be trained to become managers (in some respects learning to manage is actually doing the job), and if so, should they *all* receive management training — or just those who are particularly interested?

We believe that management training is important because there are some things which you just cannot learn by experience alone. And, having said that, as every doctor should be part of the team (albeit sometimes in a minor role), it follows that some management training is necessary for every doctor. Also, although it is not mandatory for senior registrars to have attended management courses, there can be few applying for consultant posts who would wish their curriculum vitae to be deficient in this respect.

Management courses could probably be marketed better. Some courses seem to address only a small part of what management is about, and the chosen aspect may not be seen as a need by doctors, e.g. the development of one-to-one interpersonal skills.

How much do doctors learn from management courses? They probably learn differently from managers because of the nature of undergraduate teaching, which, in the past, comprised much factual material. Concepts and role-playing teaching (familiar to business management training) are now being introduced into undergraduate medical training. Senior doctors are unaccustomed to these methods and so it is not yet clear how these concepts are best introduced.

There is a valid argument for incorporating some management training into an earlier part of a doctor's postgraduate programme, or even into the undergraduate curriculum. The move whereby senior registrars are now expected to attend management courses prior to applying for consultant posts is in the right direction and it may be that similar training should be expected of more junior staff. In our own Directorate, we include some instruction/briefing about the NHS reforms as part of our induction programme for new SHOs. Also, although the undergraduate curriculum is already overcrowded, to ignore some broad exposure to NHS changes at this level of training is an opportunity missed. Communication skills are already being introduced into the undergraduate curriculum — via OSCE examinations and by patients being assessed after interviews with students. However, the introduction of other management training has been limited. The NHS reforms have had a very cool reception by the University Deans and Professors, presumably because of their potential threat to research and the development of centres of excellence (the 'best being the enemy of the good').

How can doctors be encouraged to enthuse about management training? Insufficient attention and time have been devoted to an analysis of what is needed. The problem is now being addressed by Health Service Management Units across the country.

Peer group and the authority of the clinician in management

Why should you, as a doctor, be asked to 'manage' your colleagues? What is a Clinical Director? Why is one necessary and how has the need for such a person arisen? As a doctor–manager how would you fit in with clinical colleagues? How would you exercise any authority over them?

Whilst every clinician has a new responsibility to involve himself/herself in management, we describe here the particular problems which you will face if you take on a major management responsibility. In some organisations the doctor–manager may be expected to do nothing more than approve a course of action set by managers (i.e. the Chief Executive's team), and simply exercise a 'helmsman' role in a Clinical Directorate. At the other end of the scale is the doctor who is prepared to relinquish many clinical sessions and take on far more managerial responsibility. In our view the best medical management input can be made from a position somewhere between the two — where doctor–managers maintain most of their clinical duties and clinical status but assume some managerial duties as well. In the context of this chapter this doctor–manager will often be called a Clinical Director (CD).

Unfortunately, some doctors take on managerial duties to improve their CVs and to advance their Merit Award potential — and to further their own professional interests. In some areas the view is held that the Clinical Director is Head of Department, in which case kudos may be the reason for taking on the job rather than the need to see it done well. The right reason for doing the job is to improve the service to patients: there should be enough job satisfaction in this alone without the need for a kudos factor.

Managing doctor colleagues

There are a number of paradoxes which make it difficult to describe exactly how you can be a doctor–manager. For example, even management training may not equip you to overcome the peer group problem. What authority do you have over your clinical colleagues; how do you 'manage' a medical group where all members consider themselves equal and where each member has clinical freedom to practice as he/she chooses?

This will probably be the most difficult part of your job as a doctor in management and highlights the difference between medical and management training. Doctors are not taught motivation theories, group dynamics, etc., and management techniques have not been used extensively in medicine. One way of overcoming peer group resistance is by developing the leadership role — although even this is difficult where everyone wants to be leader. The way senior consultants have been trained is to assume leadership of a 'team' and they do not naturally work as part of a team unless they are leading it.

Although disciplinary action may be necessary, the NHS does not allow non-medical staff to be hired and fired or made redundant indiscriminately (as can happen in business). Even more difficult is the exercising of discipline over your medical colleagues if you find that they are not following, for example, agreed protocols of care, or are exceeding resource. There is no rank difference between you (as exists in the Armed Forces); nor is there a hierarchy such as exists in the Chief Executive's team. Nonetheless, you do have to manage them somehow. You have to get them to understand the management of resources and to share a vision of the Directorate's future.

The reason doctors were brought into management was that they could introduce a new dimension into developing service against resource over and above that which could be achieved by managers alone. A group of clinicians working through one advocate can facilitate this change and bring the clinical element to the fore. So, as their advocate, you have to get your colleagues to agree to a policy, a course of action.

There are ways of doing this in spite of there being no formal chain of command. These include use of the budget; peer pressure; and audit.

- *Budget*. You have a certain *right* to manage because you are *accountable* for the budget and for the quality of service. As far as financial management is concerned 'the buck stops here', i.e. on your or your Business Manager's desk.
- *Peer Pressure*. Once you have common agreement from other members of the group with whom you work in establishing a Directorate policy, colleagues who are out of line with this agreed policy will stand out and will be forced to reconsider their position.
- *Audit*. By measuring activity outcomes accurately you can demonstrate how the team should be working. A properly conducted and researched piece of work will highlight inefficiencies in your unit's current clinical management. If done properly, the results of audit cannot be argued with and cannot be ignored. Therefore, if you have to change the clinical practice of a colleague, the strongest tool you have is medical or clinical audit. Audit is discussed in detail in Chapter 4.

Example.

In one hospital the situation arose where an anaesthetist wished to use an expensive new drug for thromboprophylaxis and to charge it to a Surgical Directorate. Use of this drug was out of line with the policy agreed by the Anaesthetic Directorate but the doctor concerned invoked rights of clinical freedom to continue to use it. The surgical Clinical Director was able to stop this by witholding money from the budget.

Example.

Minimally invasive surgery (MIS) is becoming attractive because patients recover faster; they have less postoperative morbidity; they can go home earlier than after conventional (open) surgery. However, whilst there may be savings in bed usage, there are costs, e.g. the disposable tools such as staples, trocars, laser tips, used in some MIS procedures are expensive. The Clinical Director in one Surgical Unit had to put a limit on the amount of minimally invasive surgery performed by his colleagues because of the cost of disposables needed for this surgery. Proper funding had to be sought and secured before this development could proceed.

Managing nurses

As doctor–manager in a clinical specialty you may also have the responsibility for managing nursing staff. This has never before been the case in the NHS — nursing staff used to be accountable to the Senior Nursing Officer. But now you are responsible for the nursing budget and this may be the largest item of expenditure you have to control.

In reality, most aspects of day-to-day budgeting of wards and staff are delegated to Clinical Nurse Managers and Senior Ward Sisters (e.g. duty rotas, the employment of bank staff, ensuring an adequate skill mix). The management relationship between the doctor–manager and the Clinical Nurse Manager is explored later as part of the Clinical Directorate model (see p. 44). Your management has to be undertaken in a global sense with an overview of the whole Directorate. For example, sometimes the emphasis has to be shifted away from regular ward nursing staff towards the development of Nurse Specialists.

Example.

An example of professional barriers acting against the best interests of use of resources is illustrated by a Rehabilitation Directorate's development of a Rheumatology Liaison Nurse. A clinician felt that his outpatient workload could be more effectively managed if a nurse specialist post was created to deal with patients on long-term drug treatment. The resources for this post had to be 'recycled' from skill-mix changes within the general ward nursing budgets, and this was felt to be unacceptable by senior sisters on the inpatient wards. Even though the profession as a whole was benefiting from developing this expertise, the nursing staff (in general) failed to see the 'big picture' and focussed on what they saw as cutting the quality of the service they offered on the wards, in order to make life easier for the consultant! Eventually, and after some determined developmental work with key individuals, the post was created.

Negotiating such shifts in emphasis can be difficult but the trend towards nurse specialists is very strong. Employing them to undertake some duties previously done by doctors achieves a number of things: it is an excellent way of using resources — it is very cost effective, and the service provided is often better; it enlarges the role of the nurse, which should add job satisfaction and motivation; and it helps towards team-building.

The above example is typical of the resistance the doctor–manager will face, particularly in the early days of resource management. Unless you are able to motivate all key members of staff to consider the whole service before their own personal vested interests, this type of situation will recur under many different guises.

Managing other staff

Clerical and administrative staff have to be managed also. This is best done by the Business Manager, but an overview has still to be maintained by you. Working with the Business Manager, you may identify an area in your unit where changing the configuration of clerical staff would enhance the efficiency of the unit, i.e. moving staff around, deploying them in different areas and developing a multi-skilled clerical work-force.

> **Example.**
>
> A Surgical Directorate discovered that the unit would be more efficient and at the same time provide better job satisfaction if those central Medical Records Staff responsible for Surgery were devolved to the Directorate. One clerical officer became responsible for a designated area (i.e. one consultant unit). She became (i) the receptionist at that consultant's outpatient clinics; (ii) responsible for the organisation of his clinics; (iii) responsible for the retrieval of medical records for that consultant. This allowed for much more collaboration between Medical Secretaries and Records Staff and, in some areas, facilitated job-sharing. The grouping of Clerical Officer, Medical Secretary and Medical Staff within each subunit enhanced communication. The whole Directorate was easier to manage as a result.

What is management for the clinician?

For a clinician to assume a management role effectively there needs to be an understanding of the overall concept of 'management' as an art.

Management is often described (in Rosemary Stewart's (1989) words) as 'deciding what should be done and getting other people to do it' (which emphasises the 'people' aspect of management). Other definitions, such as Sir Fredrick Hooper's (Management Survey 1960), pay more attention to the 'doing' function of management, and to the manager's responsibility for achieving effective use of all resources — money, methods, materials as well as manpower.

Henry Fayol (1841–1925) put forward a classic analysis of the management task. Although he spoke from an industrial perspective, he suggested that managerial activities are universal to all organisations and consist of five elements:

- *To forecast and plan*: examining the future and drawing up a plan of action;
- *To organise*: building up the structure (material and human) of the undertaking;
- *To command*: monitoring activity among the personnel;

- *To coordinate*: binding together, unifying and harmonising all activity and effort;
- *To control*: seeing that everything occurs in conformity with established rule and expressed command.

Management theory today would, in addition to the above, stress the concepts of *individual responsibility*, and the dimension of *competitiveness*.

All managers start with a particular technical, specialist or, in this instance, clinical background, on top of which is acquired the management techniques which allow you to carry out the management processes described above. As a doctor–manager you will require a knowledge of the environment in which you work, including such factors as the effect of organisational change, conflict, motivation, power and politics.

Systems management

Doctors are unfamiliar with the concept of systems theory and management. Scientific or analytical thinking takes things apart; whereas synthetic thinking (systems) puts things together. Systems thinking concerns itself with the interaction of the relevant parts of the organised activity. It is based on the assumption that everything is part of a larger, independent arrangement and the whole is greater than the the sum of its individual parts.

Example.

A doctor looking at an outpatient facility will probably see only the doctor/patient interaction. A systems approach would take into account the patient's visit to the GP, the counselling involved at various stages, waiting time in clinics, the attitudes of nursing and clerical staff, the doctor/patient interview, and follow up through treatment or referral back to the GP (and communication arising from this), i.e. the whole network surrounding a patient's visit to a hospital outpatient clinic.

Change and how to achieve it

Change management is the most fundamental issue in the new system and in our view seems to be undervalued in the agendae of many training courses. Because doctors are extraordinarily resistant to change, courses should demonstrate the need for change and the need for clinicians' involvement in it. The management of change is discussed in Chapter 6.

Motivation skills

Ways of motivating staff — by promotion, salary rises or making their jobs more satisfying, etc. — have to be applied across the board to different staff groups. Clerical staff, medical staff and nurses will need different approaches; for example, some will not be eligible for promotion and will need an alternative motivating force.

Communication skills

The traditional one-to-one relationship that you will have developed with patients is no longer enough: today's doctor must have a wider commitment to the population of patients served by his/her unit. A more global view has to be developed.

Non-medical staff also have to understand why doctors are in this new position. A problem you will face as doctor–manager will be how to create an organisational climate where all staff understand what is going on. Clearly there needs to be a raised consciousness — across all staff — of the reason why doctors and others are being involved increasingly in management.

One way of achieving this is for Directorates to organise 'time-out' where key people on a multidisciplinary basis are taken away from the hospital to work through problems and approaches to issues. This also forms an opportunity for team building (see p. 124).

These are skills which should be covered in management courses, each is discussed in greater detail later in the book. It is important for doctors who are venturing into management to appreciate at the start the differences between medicine and management and how they may be reconciled for the common good of the service.

Administration, management and leadership

Any or all of these terms may be used in the context of the day-to-day 'management' of the Directorate. They are often used synonymously but have different meanings. Management and leadership are discussed later (see p. 46). The difference between administration and management deserves a mention here.

Administration implies orderliness and structure. Administrators give advice to policymakers and then ensure that decisions are implemented. They provide the supporting mechanism to help doctors and nurses go about the real business of the service. Few regard themselves as innovators (Stewart 1989). The NHS used to be 'administered' before Griffiths introduced management change.

Management's function is to establish processes whereby people undertand and share the corporate goals of the organisation and cooperate in achieving them. Management seeks the necessary resources and ensures that scarce ones are allocated appropriately between competing demands. Management develops communications inside and outside the organisation to ensure people are well informed.

More discussion about different types of management is presented in Chapter 6, in particular as the new emphasis in the NHS is on *leadership* rather than management alone. However, one would like to believe that characteristics of each of these managerial models are portrayed in the behaviour of each member of the Directorate management team. The Clinical Director might be seen as the transforming leader and the Business and Nurse Managers as transactional leaders or managers, although there is a considerable overlap in the behaviour of our group.

In particular, and because of the rapidly changing environment, innovative leadership from within the group as a whole is necessary for the success of the organisation. Furthermore, the effectiveness of this team leadership should not be measured by charisma, but by achievement, by the degree to which the Directorate is able to realise its planned objectives.

The job itself

Appointment of a Clinical Director

Clinical Director appointments are made in various ways and for various periods of tenure according to local conditions in individual hospitals or units. There will be common features, but it is unlikely that you would be appointed (by the Chief Executive) without the support of both the Central Management Team and a majority of your clinical colleagues. Usually there will have been a consultative period between the Chief Executive and the other members of your specialty (or specialties), during which the Chief Executive will form an opinion about who is the doctor most likely to fulfil the role best. *Pari-passu* with this process will have been discussions within the specialty Consultants to nominate one of their group. At the conclusion of these deliberations the representative (elected and nominated by his colleague specialists) should have the support of both the specialty group and the Chief Executive. At the end of the day the Chief Executive could not support anyone in whom he/she had no faith; and a Clinical Director should have a clear mandate from clinical colleagues to direct and coordinate policy in the specialty.

Job description

In our experience, job descriptions for Clinical Directors are not well developed. In our Trust, Clinical Directors have ultimate responsibility for the budget and activity of the specialty. Beyond that, responsibilities vary from being simply a 'lead doctor' in the clinical sense, to being a mini 'Chief Executive' of the service. The extent to which the styles vary is largely dependent on the abilities and inclination of the individual clinician. For that reason, Clinical Director job descriptions are not tightly formulated.

The main *disadvantage* of a detailed job description is that it may stifle innovation. The *advantages* of a clear job description are greater, for example, if the job is well-defined you will probably keep the respect of your colleagues, even if you have to delegate clinical work, e.g. shorten your clinics.

Regardless of whether or not your job description is loosely defined, there must be clear management rules defining the relative roles of the Chief Executive, the Trust Board Medical Director, yourself as Clinical Director and your consultant colleagues. Whilst service issues are your responsibility, professional issues are usually handled by a 'Three Wise Men' group. The area in between these remains grey. Whose responsibility is it, for example, to reprimand a consultant for not fulfilling a contract? These grey areas may cause you to land yourself in a difficult situation unless there is clear devolved authority from outside or above.

The best results in these situations are achieved by collaboration and understanding between the Clinical Director and the Chief Executive. It is becoming more and more clear that for the benefit of the whole organisation the joint solution to problems by cooperation between Central Management and clinician is essential.

Contract and tenure

The term of office of a Clinical Director varies between Trusts but is usually provisionally set at 3 years. The appointment may then be renewable (by agreement between Chief Executive and Consultants in the specialty) on an annual basis.

As there is a long learning curve, there may be a tendency to maintain the status quo (both by the Clinical Director and the Chief Executive). However, we believe it is important that as many people as possible are introduced to the new system as soon as possible. First, it is not possible to delegate Directorate responsibility to colleagues who do not appreciate why it is necessary; those exposed to the system are more likely to understand the pressures of combined clinical and managerial duties and are more likely to contribute their own time. Secondly, the greater the number of doctors involved in management, the faster the kudos factor will disappear and the sooner the real job will be done.

Some of the responsibility for spreading the managerial load lies with the Clinical Director who should find time to meet colleagues and to develop sideways communication. This is difficult in a busy DGH where the clinical load is great: it is almost impossible (but vital) to find a time when all consultants can meet.

Remuneration

It may be argued that insufficient resources have been given to implementing the new reforms — not necessarily for your time, but more for the provision of adequate support staff within Directorates (or whatever system operates), such as Business Manager supporting staff, secretaries and audit clerks, etc.

As far as the pay of the Clinical Director is concerned, it has been assumed in some hospitals that the role can be discharged within *one* extra session per week. In others, two sessions have been allocated but even this may be unrealistic for large Clinical Directorates with budgets in excess of £5m. This scale of financial responsibility is similar to that of a medium-sized private business. In other units, Clinical Directors are rewarded on results rather than the time spent doing the job, e.g. by lump sum payments. Unfortunately, because clinical work has to continue (after all, this is your job and you have to return to it afterwards — and you have also to maintain credibility with your colleagues), much of the work has to be squeezed into any available time during the day — and then the rest is taken home.

Example.

In one Trust, Clinical Directors were paid one session for their extra work. When a badly-timed move to marginally increase Clinical Director remuneration reached the press, the reaction was more vitriolic amongst clinical colleagues than from lay personnel, indicating how limited was the understanding amongst many senior medical staff of the extent of management involvement by Clinical Directors.

Even amongst senior doctors there is as yet little appreciation of the extent of change that has happened in the NHS, and of its exponential character. Clinicians who are prepared to take on the management of this change at the expense of their clinical development, research interests, private lives and private practice — and are able to do so with the required verve and commitment, are doing their colleagues an immense service which thus far has been grossly underestimated.

Key relationships

Central Executive Team

It is important to have good working relationships with the Chief Executive and the Chief Finance Officer. These can best be achieved by fulfilling your management role to their satisfaction, i.e. keeping to your business plan and managing your budget. It is unlikely that the Chief Executive Team will withdraw support and recentralise budgetary management, but you are likely to receive less favourable treatment from the Central Team (and in particular from the Finance Department) if you do your job badly.

Hospital Council and Trust Board

At the time of writing there are 13 Clinical Directorates in our Hospital Trust. The Hospital Council, the hospital's key governing body for operational issues, comprises the 13 Clinical Directors and the Chief Executive Team of officers.

As with a large number of committees, much of the decision-making is based on background discussion before and outside the meeting. This happens with the Hospital Council Meetings also. Informal discussions about areas of concern can be mutually beneficial, and, of course, will speed the business of Hospital Council.

When you have been a Clinical Director for some time you should be in a position to state clearly to the Chief Executive where unresolved financial pressures exist. By now you can tell whether these are due to bad management, underfunding, or promised funds not materialising. The rapport with the Chief Executive should be sufficiently established that you can say (and be believed) that without central help something cannot be accomplished and it cannot be expected of your Directorate. Informal meetings with the Chief Executive or the other members of the Central Executive Team (and with the Trust Board members) should also be used to detail the future changes envisaged in your Directorate, i.e. to share the vision of the future with these groups also.

Business and Clinical Nurse Managers

The key relationships for the Clinical Director with Business and Clinical

Nurse Managers are described later as part of the Clinical Directorate model (see p. 44).

Other Directorates

Dividing the hospital services into individual Directorates, each with responsibility for its own budget can, to some extent, introduce a 'tribal' culture into the hospital, making relationships with other service areas more difficult. This is highlighted particularly where a Directorate may be struggling to manage a budget, but does not have direct control of the users of its services (e.g. operating theatres and pathology, which are demand led).

Difficulties have arisen when the activity of demand-led specialties (e.g. Pathology, Anaesthetics) is increased, e.g. by a successful waiting list initiative bid. Surgical specialties have had to attract waiting list initiative money in order to reduce excessively long waiting lists. Bidding successfully for this money is difficult enough but even harder is motivating colleagues in affected non-surgical specialties.

Because of the need to obtain support from these specialties (e.g. Theatres and Anaesthetics), an internal market has developed within the hospital. Negotiation is needed to establish each specialty's share of the allocated amount.

Example.

In one hospital, the Theatres Directorate declared Unilateral Declaration of Independence in an attempt to manage an excessive overspend. Operating sessions were severely curtailed, which had a dramatic and detrimental effect on the surgical specialties. The Chief Executive could not allow this to happen and had to intervene for the greater good of the whole hospital.

Establishing good working relationships with some Directorates is not always easy, although when collaboration is possible it can be very useful. For example, the Surgical Directorates (e.g. General Surgery, Gynaecology, Orthopaedics and other Surgical Specialties) have similar resource managerial problems such as reducing outpatient waiting times and inpatient waiting lists. In many instances it is possible and useful to compare notes on how best to manage these problems.

Until now, most of us have been concerned mainly with the internal problems of resource management, the setting and balancing of budgets and reducing waiting lists, and there has been little time for much else. But as far as future development is concerned, the 'tribal culture' is likely to impede inter-Directorate *innovative* collaboration. Some Clinical

Directors seem to have a better vision of the future than others with whom any collaborative project is extremely difficult: some only concern themselves with the present and its problems and you cannot influence them with pictures of a better future in the same way as you can your own workforce.

Example.

A key relationship for an O&G Directorate was with the Department of Radiology (with whom there were conflicting views on the future of ultrasound services in Obstetrics). This centred around a vision which the O&G Directorate had for a self-contained Obstetric Ultrasound Unit. The view was that this would be mutually beneficial to the two departments, but this view was not shared by Radiology, mainly because of staff deployment problems. This has now been solved by the O&G Directorate taking on a part-time radiographer.

A further solution to this problem was to enlist the help of GP fundholders who were keen to have direct access to obstetric ultrasound facilities. An extra ultrasonographer was funded from this source.

The provision of anaesthetic cover may be outside the control of the Surgical Directorates and even though it may be an anaesthetic shortage that curtails elective operating time, the Surgical Directorates are the ones who suffer the patients' and relatives' complaints about waiting times. Pressures are being exerted from the Government, the Central Executive Group, the Community Health Council and now the Patients' Charter, to reduce waiting lists. This is very frustrating and demoralising. This sort of pressure generates animosity between Directorates and impedes progress.

The framework

Development of the Clinical Directorate system at Arrowe Park Hospital

The chronological sequence of NHS reforms has varied from one hospital and health authority to the next. Our experience is from a hospital that was one of the pilot sites for the Resource Management Initiative (RMI). Here, Trust status came after Clinical Directorates and the Hospital Council model (see below) were already well established. In other hospitals, the onset of Trust status has highlighted the need for Clinical Directorates, so they have developed at a later stage, in others Medical Directors representing the whole of the medical staff group of a hospital have been incorporated into the Trust Board (whilst still maintaining clinical practice), and yet seem to be performing the same functions as Clinical Directors. In others, the Clinical Directorship role appears to have been assumed simply to conform, without there being a sincere interest in the success or development of the organisation (in this case the Directorate). So the observed clinical/management structure will be different in other parts of the country and we can only describe the changes we have experienced. Other units will, no doubt, adapt in their own ways to the new system and will find solutions different from ours to similar problems.

Even in our hospital the management structure has changed dramatically since we began to write this book. It is almost impossible to document anything on NHS reorganisation that is completely up-to-date, and we can only describe the events as we have experienced them during a small window of time.

Whilst at the beginning there was a clear directive for clinicians to link with management, there were no rules or guidelines on how to do it. In 1987/1988, management in this hospital was beginning to assemble itself around a core group of Clinical Directors. The plan was that Central Hospital Management should devolve much of its responsibility to a group of Clinical Directors each of whom sat on a Hospital Council. The Council would have, as its Chairman, the Unit General Manager (now known as the Chief Executive). He/she would have a small team of close advisers, including his/her immediate Deputy, the Director of Finance, the Site Manager and the Senior Nurse of the hospital (Fig. 2.1). As the managerial responsibilities of senior nursing staff became more centred in the Clinical Directorate, the role of the Director of Nursing Services changed (except for professional issues). In our Hospital Council, this person has now become the Operational Manager and Head of Quality Control.

The executive group of the hospital was the Hospital Council, comprising 13 Clinical Directors and the Chief Executive's team. This system (with minor modifications) is still in operation although the hospital is now an NHS Trust (Fig. 2.2). In our hospital, the Trust Board is very unobtrusive and non-invasive in management decisions. Discussion at Hospital Council usually leads to agreement about hospital policy.

The changing role of senior nursing management was probably the greatest culture shock: overnight, nurses who had been senior in managerial terms were now responsible to a clinician rather than to the Divisional Nursing Officer (previously the 'Matron') — and many of them found this hard to accept (the previous lines of command remained incompletely severed for some time: there remained a subservience to the old order and a resistance to change).

Some senior nurses could see themselves without an effective job in

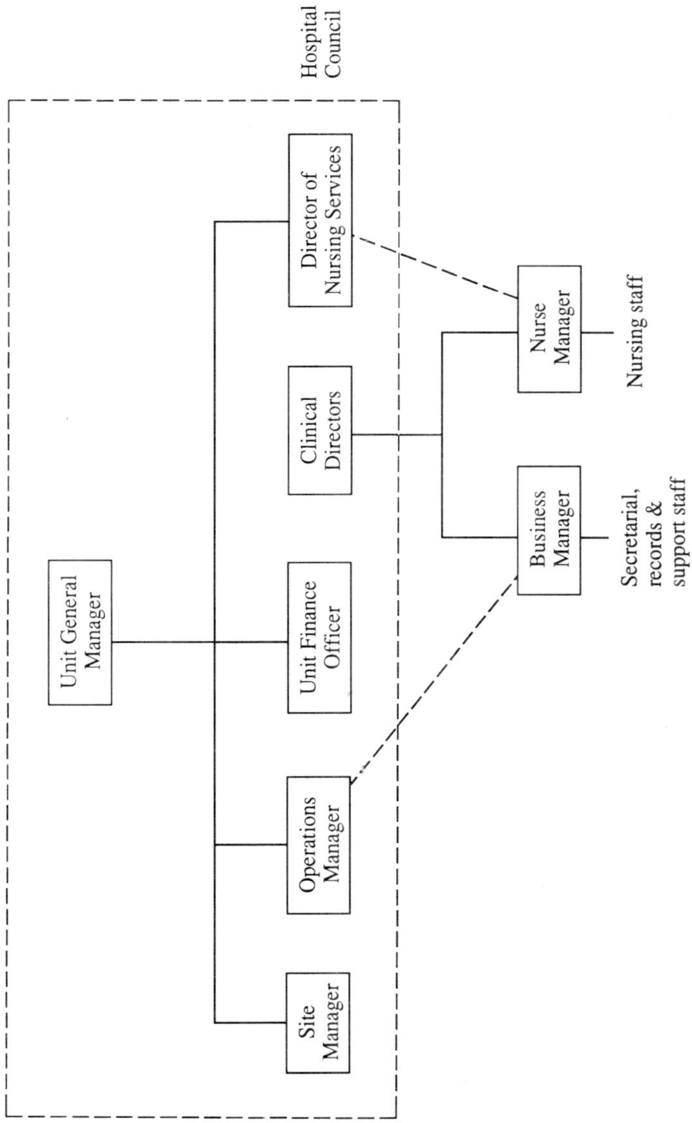

Figure 2.1 An early model of Directorate relationship with Unit General Management

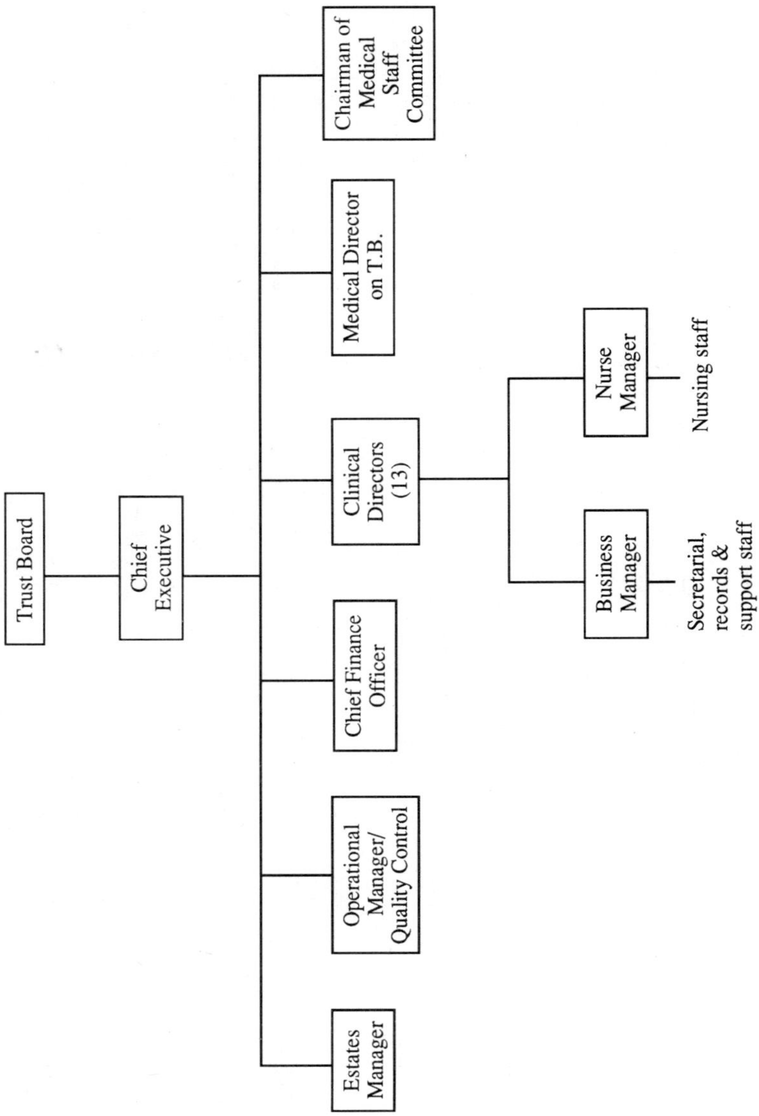

Figure 2.2 Relationships of Directorates within a Trust

the new system. Some indicated a wish to become Business Managers in Clinical Directorates. This was not an unreasonable direction for them to follow: the nursing budget in any hospital is the largest item of expenditure; the nursing workforce is the largest group in the NHS. Managing these two in any Directorate is a major undertaking.

However, some nurses have been able successfully to combine general management with managing nursing. In other instances the emerging demands on the Clinical Director brought an acknowledgement that there were managerial skills necessary to run an effective Directorate which were not currently being supplied by the Nurse Manager/Clinical Director combination. An additional degree of managerial support was necessary.

It was unclear what form this should take. Junior administrative support might be nothing more than that which already existed in the NHS. But this was a new management system in which it was recommended that senior management be involved at all levels. If managerial responsibility was to be devolved to the 'face-workers', then so should senior managers. A number of Clinical Directors agreed that there was a need for a senior management person working alongside the Clinical Director and a Senior Nurse. Whilst appreciating the need for professional nursing advice, there was a need also for a pure Business/Operational Manager. In other words, the 'management' system inside each Directorate should be a sort of triumvirate with each member bringing into that team his/her own clinical and managerial skills (Fig. 2.3). For most Clinical Directorates in the Wirral Hospital Trust, this model has proved to be the most useful.

Other models

Our organisational system is based on the Johns Hopkins' model and is very similar to the one adopted at Guy's Hospital. Other systems devised to involve and support doctors in management have been designed with the same objective, namely to simplify communications/relationships and accountability between the central managers and the service or specialty managers. Figure 2.4 is a variation seen in some Trusts. This model has two senior doctors reporting to the Chief Executive, a Director of Medical Services and a Director of Surgical Services.

Community care

The *Cultural Revolution* report of the Audit Commission (1992) identifies areas that are critical to Community Care Reforms. They are much the same as the cultural changes required inside the acute sector, namely:

- committed leadership;
- establishment of clear values and goals;
- devolved budgeting; tackling community care as a corporate issue;
- resource management and allocation;
- prioritising care.

Community Health Services are provided and managed by NHS Trusts (or DMUs) and include the provision of:

- health centres (not GP health centres);
- district nurses;
- health visitors;
- chiropody; family planning clinics, etc.

All these lie in the primary care sector and there is overlap between their provision by Trusts and similar care provided by GPs and practice nurses. The doctor–manager in this arena may be expected to have a

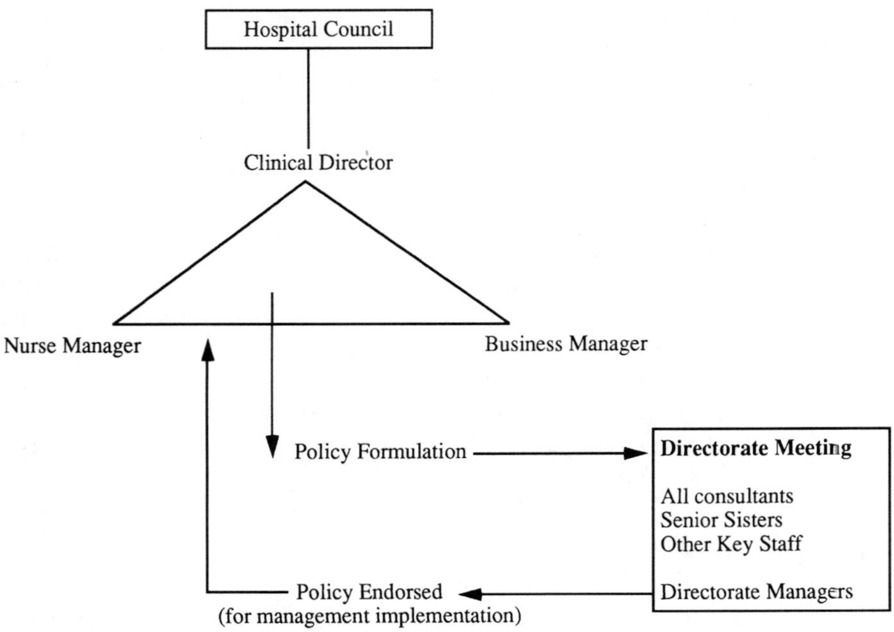

Figure 2.3 The Directorate triumvirate and its relationships

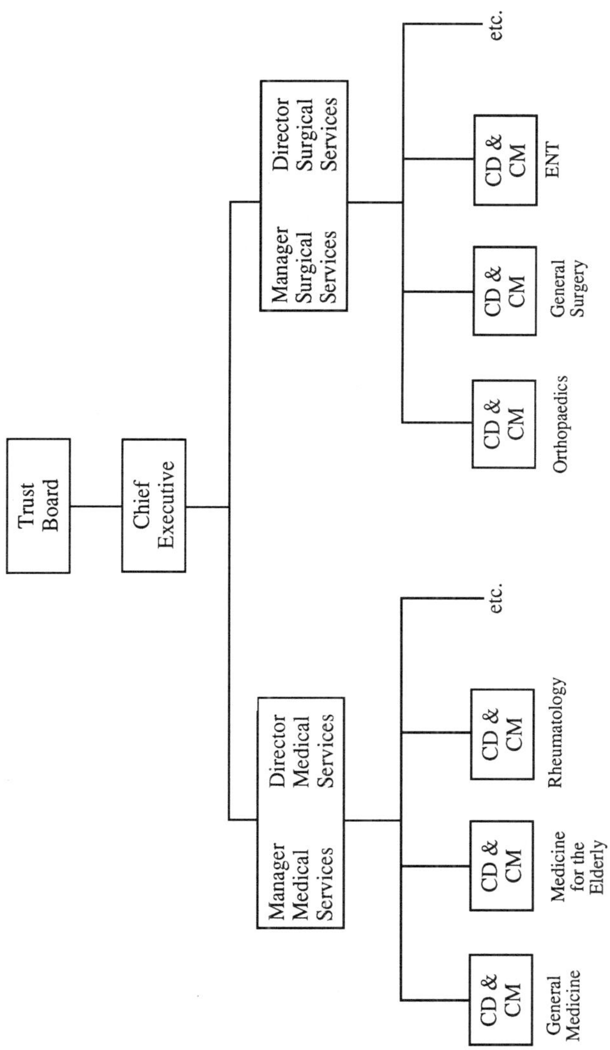

CD = Clinical Director
CM = Clinical Manager

Figure 2.4 An alternative Trust model

major coordinating role in the provision of primary care. There is a danger that without this coordination patients will fall between two services.

The differences between this arena and the acute hospital relate mainly to communication/coordination with services outside the NHS with which doctor–managers in community care need to work more closely. The number of staff and size of budget for Community Health Services will be smaller than for hospital Trusts, but may be spread across several sites and involve contracts with agencies outside the NHS, e.g. with Housing, Social Services, and voluntary agencies.

The Clinical Director is likely to be a specialist in Mental Health, Medicine for the Elderly or Psychiatry. Relationships with an executive group will be the same but there will also be a greater role for organisations outside the NHS.

The difficulty is the overlap between Community Health Services provided by NHS Trusts and care provided by GPs and practice nurses. The Clinical Directorate organisation in a CHS must recognise its coordinating role with other providers — and purchasers — of primary care. An emerging proposition is some form of joint health and social care commissioning (Hudson 1993).

Another major function of community units is agreeing and implementing arrangements for discharging patients from acute hospitals and for providing them with care in the community.

Directorate Management Team

Directorates have adopted different styles of organisation for day-to-day Directorate management, largely dependent on the style and priorities of the Director. At the start the organisational structure within our Directorate was as follows. A 'central' management team comprising Clinical Director, Business Manager and Clinical Nurse Manager would meet at least once a week to identify operational issues needing further attention, either by working groups or by referral to the Directorate Forum.

The speed of change being what it is, the composition of the Directorates in this hospital has undergone modification since we started writing this book. The Business and Nurse Managers' roles have been subsumed by that of a 'generic' Business Manager, whose role is therefore strengthened (and salary increased) and who may have responsibilities in more than one Directorate. It is too early to say whether or not the new arrangements will work. Ostensibly they have been made to streamline the service, but probably also to give the Chief Executive more control through the stronger business link. Clearly, proper recognition of the value of a dedicated and committed Business Manager is welcomed, but the move will potentially dilute the strength of the Clinical Director.

Below we describe the structure with which we have been familiar for 4–5 years and return to some discussion about managerial changes in the final chapter of the book.

The Directorate Management Team (DMT) acts as an agenda committee for the Directorate meetings which are held monthly. There is always an element of day-to-day crisis and reactive management which this group has to handle: in medicine there seems to be no way of avoiding this.

The management group is the link between Hospital Council and the Directorate Forum (Fig. 2.3), from which information cascades down (via nominated officers) to all members of the Directorate.

Directorate Forum

The Directorate Forum is attended by all the Consultant staff, an Associate Specialist, a Senior Registrar (who also represents the junior staff — at their request), all senior sisters in gynaecology and all managerial sisters in maternity, and the Business Manager. A recent addition is a GP representative who is also the GP Postgraduate Tutor for the District and a partner in a fundholding practice. Other key staff are coopted when necessary (e.g. Chief Pharmacist, Finance Department staff).

There was potential conflict in this configuration. If all the Senior Sisters in Midwifery had been invited to attend, the committee would have been overwhelmed and top-heavy in Maternity representation. Gynaecology Nurse representation is at a lower level, but there are far less of them and they do need a voice — there is no equivalent to the Maternity Advisory Committee in Gynaecology. The present composition was agreed after discussion and appears to work well.

By and large the business of this committee is to discuss major policy changes and developments. Also, Unit policy decided at Hospital Council is translated into potential Directorate policy by the DMT and brought to the Directorate Forum for debate. The policy is amended or endorsed and conveyed back to Council. As the Directorate grows in strength and management experience there is less need to involve Central Management in decision-making. The Directorate should become more self-sufficient and needs increasingly less support from outside.

There are a number of other committees which are not necessarily executive. In O&G there are two: the Maternity Advisory Committee (MAC) and the Maternity Liaison Committee (MLC) (Fig. 2.5). We have found it helpful clearly to define the functions of each of these. The

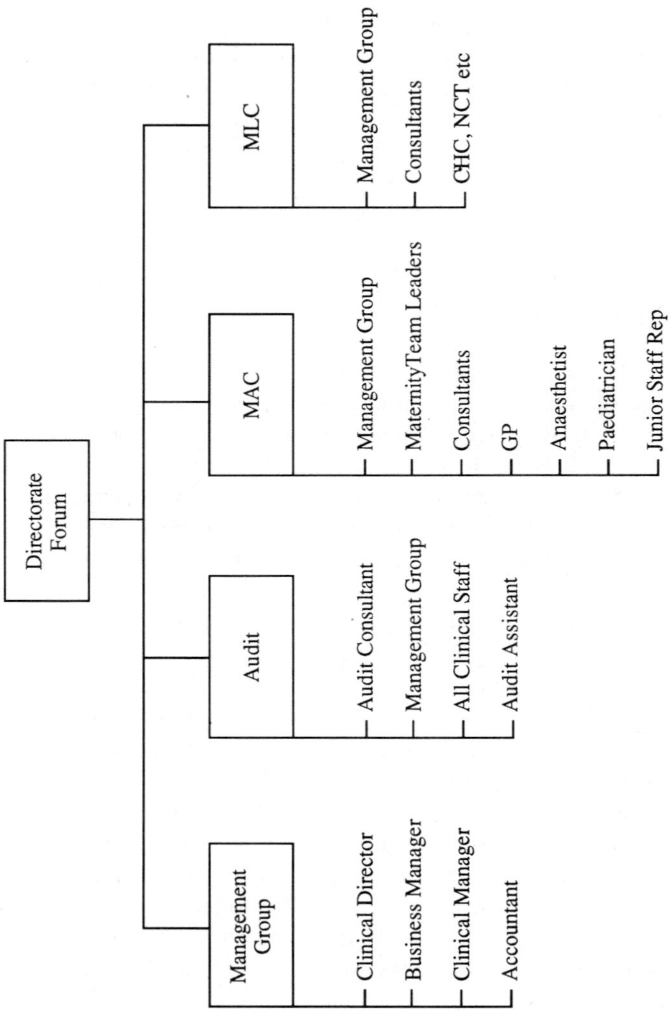

Figure 2.5 The communication structure within the Arrowe Park O & G Directorate

Directorate Forum is the only executive one: its composition and functions are described above. The MAC is statutory but not executive. It is an advisory committee which meets once every 2 months. Its function is to devise and compile protocols. This is a larger group reflecting the representation needed for the new move towards team midwifery. Included in its membership are a GP representative, a Consultant Anaesthetist and a Consultant Paediatrician. The MLC (also statutory), is larger still in its representation, and includes members of the Community Health Council, the National Childbirth Trust, etc. This committee meets only twice a year. We try to parcel all the major meetings into 1 day each month.

The objective throughout is to give everyone in the organisation a chance for his/her voice to be heard, whilst keeping the executive group as small and effective as possible. Of course, there has to be an efficient system of cascade of information down the tree as well as representation upwards.

An Audit Group meets once a month (as prescribed by the Audit Commission). One of the consultants is in charge of the audit programme and reports to the Hospital Audit Committee. However, it is felt that medical audit is such an integral part of Directorate function that it should come under the umbrella of the Clinical Directorate. Otherwise there is a danger that two systems will work in parallel but not be coordinated. It has been agreed that subject matter for audit be discussed and decided at the Directorate Forum and that reports from the Audit Consultant be given regularly to that committee.

Directorate's needs

For a Clinical Directorate to function effectively it needs:

- a means of managing staff;
- an information system;
- professional nursing advice;
- a means of forward planning and evaluation of performance;
- a communication system;
- an administrative/organisational system;
- a means by which it can assess, on a continuous basis, the quality of patient care (see Chapter 4).

Some of these functions have been covered or briefly described above.

Staff management, both clinical and non-clinical is the responsibility of the central management triumvirate. The roles of the Business and Nurse Managers are described below.

The availability of reliable and up-to-date information in the NHS has always been poor. This compromises the bargaining power of the DMT and without it everything has to be calculated manually. In this Region, activity data from 2–3 years ago are still being circulated as if relevant to the present. At a time when GP fundholders are shopping around for the best deal for their patients it is of vital importance to the provider units to have data which can realistically be compared with other units.

Inside the Trust itself information on each specialty's activity, throughput, waiting list status, etc., is now becoming essential and so we are able to construct accurate business plans and evaluate up to date performance.

Roles of Business Manager and Nurse Manager

The Business Manager and Nurse Manager deal with operational issues on a day-to-day basis, troubleshoot, develop and see through agreed initiatives. Their principal responsibilities are to:

- Manage the budget (with the Nurse Manager being largely responsible for the nursing budget and the Business Manager for the non-nursing budget);
- Assist in the operational management of the Directorate;
- Collect, analyse and present information on Directorate performance (financial, manpower and activity) to enable informed decisions to be taken about the management of the Directorate;
- Perform the business planning function for the Directorate — including research and feasibility studies for new projects and projected activity and financial and costing profiles;
- Manage and be accountable for the non-clinical (Business Manager) and clinical (Nurse Manager and Clinical Director) staff employed in the Directorate;
- Organise communication processes and systems within the Directorate and with the Health Authority and general public;
- Ensure good personnel and industrial relations practices;
- Develop cost-improvement programmes and coordinate income generation schemes;

- Liaise with the appropriate managers in the implementation use and development of Patient Care Information Systems;
- In conjunction with the Clinical Director, establish overall Directorate quality standards;
- In conjunction with the Clinical Director and Senior Registrar, establish control mechanisms for junior medical staff;
- Facilitate the evaluation of Directorate performance against agreed objectives.

In some Directorates these responsibilities may be largely assumed by the Business Manager; in others by the Clinical Nurse Manager. In any event there is a large element of overlap between their responsibilities (Table 2.1).

The Nurse Manager has the major responsibility of managing the nursing budget. As nurses comprise the largest staff group in the NHS they consume a large part of each Clinical Directorate's budget, so the task is not easy, particularly where the Directorate is small and there is

Table 2.1 Overlap of responsibilities between Nurse and Business Manager

Nurse Manager	Business Manager
Recruitment, selection, etc. of nursing staff	Recruitment, etc. of clerical and support staff
Managing the nursing budget and other financial areas related to nursing	Managing non-nursing budget and areas, with definition of systems of control and analysis for total budget
Administration relating to nurses	Administrative organisation of Directorate
Communication relating to nurses	Directorate communication
Professional nursing standards	Professional management advice, organisational and systems analysis, business planning
Evaluation of nursing performance	Evaluation of Directorate performance

little room to manoevre. He/she also has the professional responsibilities of maintaining nursing standards and evaluating performance, recruiting and selecting staff.

From the nurses' point of view, there may be certain dilemmas associated with being managed by someone who is not a nurse — mainly because a Nurse Manager is governed by the United Kingdom Central Council (UKCC) Code of Conduct, as are all nurses, but doctors and managers are not tied to the same system. In our Directorate we are fortunate in having a very senior nurse (the Principal Midwife) as part of the Directorate management team.

How to do it

What makes a successful Clinical Director?

Leadership

You need to be a *transformational* leader rather than a *transactional* manager. You need sufficient leadership skills to overcome the peer group dilemma and to manage nurses and other staff. As leader you should have clear personal values and standards by which to work. People working alongside you must know what you are doing and why you are doing it. You cannot push your own needs ahead of others.

Vision

You need to have a long-term focus and a broad view on the progress of your department, i.e. you should have a vision of the future 5–10 years hence. This is more than the skill needed to manage the present (which is also necessary); you should have ideals for the future and *where* you want to lead your group rather than *how*.

Common goal

Your main function as doctor–manager is to use your skills to persuade, cajole, coax and sometimes negotiate the rest of the team into a position where they are all pointing (in terms of the future of the unit) in the same direction; i.e. they all share your vision of the future. You have to overcome inertia in the system. The *group* has to be gathered and motivated to work as a cohesive force with a common goal.

This must be a subtle and long-term process. The whole workforce must see that by the creative use of resources (or virement, i.e. shifting items from one budget heading to another) they can all be helped. They will not have seen the budget in action before; and even if they have, the way a budget can be managed now is far different from before — each Directorate can set priorities in its business plan and visibly achieve them. This can be described as a 'win–win' situation, where there is something in it for everyone. As far as possible, the staff should feel that whatever is established as part of these negotiations derives from their achievements.

Example.

The colposcopy section of an oncology unit was having to operate in cramped , poorly ventilated rooms. By identifying the need for better provision for this service as top priority in the Directorate business plan, resources were able to be directed towards the establishment of a purpose-built colposcopy unit with the commensurate devolution of staff in that direction.

Business planning

Business planning is discussed in Chapter 3. However, it deserves brief mention here because you, in collaboration with your Business Manager, need good business planning to be successful. As doctor–manager you and your Business Manager should be able to address questions such as:

- What are the major trends in the way our specialty is moving and what is their significance for the Directorate? What services should we be developing now?
- How should we be reacting (now and in the future) to the new reforms, GP fundholding, etc.? How can our unit sell itself better? How will our performance be measured?
- What will happen if we do not change? What will be the early warning signals that will cause us to change direction?
- What are the critical external events that may happen in the near future? How do we change internally to make the most of opportunities as they present?

To avoid conflict by the reactive management of short-term problems, part of your role as doctor–manager is to secure agreement with colleagues about the future and to develop a shared vision, so there is an overlap between business management as a *skill* and vision of the future as a *quality*.

Support of colleagues may be more easily obtained if you are responsible for a single specialty. It will be more difficult if you have a group of specialties to manage. It appears that many hospitals are moving towards Directorate groupings, producing a smaller number of lead clinicians with consolidated management arrangements. Whilst this may streamline the way in which the whole hospital functions, the doctor taking the lead over a number of clinical areas has a difficult job. Whilst it may be relatively easy to pull together consultants who have a common interest, it is likely to be far more difficult to manage a group of specialties.

Budgetary control: resource management and allocation

You must work alongside the other members of the Directorate management team in managing and allocating resources. Whilst you may have intuitive skills in listening to people, diagnosing problems, etc., you may understand less about contracting or marketing the services which the unit has to offer.

In 40 years of the NHS, there has been no adequate system for pricing different specialties — let alone pricing individual treatments. The NHS has never needed to be a business 'financially'. In business accurate costing has always been necessary for survival whereas in the NHS all that was needed was for the hospital to know how much it was spending and how much it was being given by the government. Suddenly, the NHS has been expected to assume a 'business' format, and this is proving to be very difficult.

Because the financial system is in transition from a central financial accounting system to a devolved (specialty) one, there may be little reliable data upon which to base budgetary decisions. You have to rely heavily on the financial skills of the Business Manager. Working at 'coal-face' level, the Business Manager has to appreciate the financial difficulties and constraints facing a Directorate.

Part of the resource management/allocation process is the setting of objectives for the financial year, constructing a business plan and meeting the targets, etc., within the constraints of your budget. The management model with which people are most familiar is an inward-looking process where the aim of management is to use financial and technical resources to provide services which people want as economically as possible. A useful tool for analysing the tasks/problems encountered in the job is a closed-loop system. One or more closed-loop systems may be introduced where error messages are identified and the error corrected. The sequence of events is:

(a) identification of errors in the system;
(b) setting objectives/targets to correct them;
(c) establishing criteria for success;
(d) developing a strategy and policy for undertaking it;
(e) comparing target with performance.

Such tools are discussed in greater detail in Chapter 3.

Power and how to 'exploit it'

The title of Clinical Director gives you some power—it carries with it the authority to manage money, resources, and possibly the promotion of others. Also, to have been voted into the job, it is likely that you are already well-respected by your peers. Seniority adds to this formula. The combination of these generates a great deal of power. Of course, you then have to learn how to use it to influence people and negotiate but this power base is a sound negotiating platform.

As doctor–manager you should know where other sources of power exist and how to tap them. You may have to work through various contacts and channels and sometimes there are different routes to solving a problem.

1. *Chief Finance Officer*. As discussed above, it is useful to have a good working relationship with the Chief Finance Officer. It may sometimes be possible, through him/her, to present a special case of need and gain extra resource.

Example.

In one hospital a Clinical Director, with the help of the Chief Finance Officer, was able to secure funding for a Research Fellowship. It was agreed that, because the Research Fellow would provide some emergency cover (and thereby reduce the on-call locum bill), the Directorate budget would part-fund the post. Because the job would have a substantial service commitment (thereby enabling the reduction of junior doctors' hours), the post would be part-funded centrally.

2. *Personnel Departments*. Most of the information you will need about non-medical staffing will be available from the personnel department via the Business Manager or Clinical Nurse Manager (or Service Manager), but sometimes you will have to act more directly using a different route.

> **Example.**
>
> One District advertised for a Continence Adviser (the first in the District) but did not appreciate the need for someone of senior grade in this post. Only when the Clinical Director, via contacts in the Continence Adviser Association, realised how badly the job was being advertised were changes made (via the then Chief of Personnel). A top-grade Continence Adviser was appointed.

3. *GP fundholders.* Another source of funding for nursing or paramedical staff may be the purchasing bodies. GPs are anxious to foster developments in the interface between primary and secondary care, e.g. community nurse projects, and may be prepared to fund them.
4. *Purchasing Authorities.* Later in this chapter we describe how a community need for a better termination of pregnancy service led to the development of a well-constructed pregnancy counselling service. On this occasion close rapport was necessary with the DHA purchasing consortium. Important purchaser contact points are the Chairman of the local FHSA, the District GP Tutor and the Executive Team of the DHA.
5. *Regional Health Authority.* Audit is a programme for which there is separate Government funding but when seeking financial or staffing assistance for audit, it is a wise move to ask for advice from the RHA, through which all requests have to be processed anyway, rather than relying entirely on your local hospital machinery.
6. *Royal Colleges and Universities.* For medical staff appointments you need contacts at Royal College and RHA levels, and within your local university (Postgraduate Deans are becoming extremely powerful people!).

> **Example.**
>
> One hospital was able to secure the appointment of a Senior Registrar — against a lot of competition — largely because of close liaison with the Postgraduate Dean with regard to the job description, and similar liaison with one of the Royal Colleges with regard to job content, the timing of the application, etc.

Management issues

Over and above your leadership role and the attention that needs to be given to the budget and activity, there are a number of other issues which you cannot avoid. They relate to common-or-garden subjects such as the following:

1. *Unexpected deadlines.* You will receive frequent requests for reports (e.g. on activity); for responses from your group of consultants to health service directives and protocols; for responses to GPs' enquiries about your Directorate's functions. Many of the medico-legal and other complaints requiring reports will be channelled through your office, even though the staff concerned have long since left the hospital. All of these are usually needed within 24–48 hours. These reports are very disruptive to any time management plan you have but cannot be ignored because of you and your Business Manager's accountability to Central Management.

> **Example.**
>
> The requests from the Chief Executive team for reports and evaluations often relate to activity data several years old. Correcting and justifying these data are recurrent problems — unless you do it immediately you can be sure that incorrect data will be presented to the general public, GPs, the rest of the Region etc.

2. *Medical staff.* You will find yourself responsible for the compilation of shortlists; the organisation of interviews; and the selection of junior staff. With the District Tutor you will need to concern yourself with job descriptions, recruitment and the development of a successful induction programme for new junior doctors; with their hours of duty; and with their postgraduate training. The search for locums can be delegated but their cost is your responsibility. You will need to approve holiday, professional and study leave and ensure (through delegation) that service functions are covered. You will need to submit bids, job descriptions and timetables for new staff. You will be the one expected to liaise most closely with GPs and fundholders.

3. *Counselling/career advice.* A regular, day-to-day part of your job is to offer advice to present and past staff members about career guidance, references, testimonials, etc. You also have to listen to staff grievances, work problems, etc. You must provide good quality listening time. Sometimes reprimands and disciplinary action are needed. For non-medical staff this is usually the territory of the Business Manager, Nurse Manager or other line manager but you will be expected to counsel junior medical staff and sometimes nursing staff with regard to substandard performance. Most problems (e.g. complaints from patients) arise because of a lack of communication or some personality clash between nurse/doctor and patient. In a large organisation with a high throughput of patients and a rapid turnover of staff these events are bound to happen.

They are mostly trivial but should all be taken seriously because situations can degenerate very fast.

Your role as doctor–manager is to spot behaviour which is happening or not happening, and to seek specialist help if necessary. There are good reasons for medical/business managers to take responsibility for handling all 'people problems' at the level of least formality, which means that, in the main, you have to do it personally.

4. *Nursing staff.* You will need to understand how the shortage of nurse learners affects your ward practice; what bank staff requirements are; the difficulties of nurse recruitment; and how the incremental drift in salaries affects your budget. Your long-term plans must include provision for Specialist Nurses. Your short-term management issues must include an understanding of why Health Care Assistants might (in some cases) be more appropriate than qualified nurses in the Outpatient clinics.

5. *Equipment.* You will need to submit updated equipment bids on a regular basis; argue your case in equipment committees, approach other potential sources of income such as WRVS and the League of Friends. As part of your long-term plans you must consider subspecialty developments and the equipping of such units.

6. *Audit.* Although you will have an audit specialist in your group of consultants, you should still have an overview of the audit programme and be able to monitor it through the Directorate system. It is likely that you will be the person bidding for audit assistance, computer software and staff, because you know the resource available in your budget and what additional help is needed to fund extra staff.

7. *Information technology.* The learning curve for computerised patient administration systems and other technology is long. Motivating staff to use it is hard, particularly when there are no immediate benefits. Information systems are discussed on p. 56.

8. *General hospital problems.* Any points of contention about outpatient waiting times and inpatient waiting times, anaesthetic and theatre time and bed management will come directly to you for solution. You must ensure that your internal Directorate management systems are constructed to address these problems.

Example.

Large DGHs face an immense problem with bed management in the winter months when there is a large influx of General Medical emergencies. Surgical wards may be expected to take outliers if there are no medical beds; specialties like Gynaecology which have small numbers of beds are most vulnerable because a relatively small influx of medical cases can virtually wipe out the next day's surgical admissions. Clearly, there is no way an emergency admission can be turned away if there is a spare bed in the hospital, but it is known that some specialties still operate a 'hot-bed' policy and that others continue to admit routine 'cold' cases even though they have outliers. A Working Party comprising Clinical Directors of the most-affected specialties was convened in one hospital to address this problem and recommended certain actions, including the insistance that Medical specialties 'consume their own smoke' whenever possible, 'hot-bed' policies be discouraged and that a bed-bureau system be established. The bed-bureau recommendation went ahead (but bed-bureau managers can easily be manipulated by a shrewd registrar!). Most of the recommendations were ignored. By the time people have really addressed the problem it will be summer and the crisis will be over, only to be resurrected again next year.

9. *General managerial problems.* You have to deploy clerical and secretarial staff in different ways that best suit the structure and functions of the department. You may have to supervise doctors' timetables, theatre lists, cross charging issues. You will have to make decisions on performance-related pay returns for managerial staff. The Business Manager will do most of this, but you will have to assist in the writing of the Directorate's business plan and the monitoring of departmental progress against objectives.

10. *Building bridges.* One of the more important parts of your job as doctor–manager is bridging the gap between management, clinical medicine and nursing, i.e. overcoming the 'them and us' mentality. Only you can bring these groups together so that they can work alongside each other without suspicion.

Meetings

Function and importance

It is important to be clear about the function and relative importance of different meetings and committees. Some are advisory, some executive. Some are a waste of time; others you cannot afford to miss.

Attendance at senior meetings (e.g. Hospital Council) is part of your job. Strategic decisions are taken here. It is important not to default these meetings not only because you need to follow what is going on in the main organisation (the Hospital or Trust), but also to contribute to the corporate management programme and to present your Directorate's case for, say, development schemes. Also, in spite of the Council being a corporate-minded body of clinicians and managers, you have always to be there to state your Directorate's case.

The agenda

For internal (Directorate) meetings you are in charge of the agenda. Much can be achieved outside the formal meeting and only important items which cannot be dealt with elsewhere should be considered. They should be prioritised so that sufficient time can be devoted to the main topics. Even then there should be a guillotine on the meeting if it extends beyond a certain time. It is preferable to state in advance that a meeting will end at a certain time.

This is not to say that all meetings should be rushed through at great speed: committee members must have an opportunity to air their views and to contribute to the discussion, particularly those representing a large number of people and those with relevant information. They should be allowed to feel that they are part of the team. A good chairman will invite contributions from those who seem diffident.

However, some people just like to hear themselves talk and raise objections to everything. Theirs are not usually constructive criticisms and serve only to stifle a meeting. Such people are very predictable and their criticisms can usually be anticipated. So, having answers to their potential objections in advance and immediately to hand goes a long way towards smoothing the progress of the meeting.

Minutes

Given the speed of change and limited time available for discussion and implementation of decisions/plans, the age of minute keeping is over. We think that minutes should be abolished!

The speed of change resulting from the NHS reforms makes the traditional meeting format clumsy. It should be radically revised. 'Nit-picking' through the minutes of the last meeting precludes discussion on relevant topics of the day (it is a tactic used by people who want to hinder change). At present the system is changing so fast that issues on last month's agenda are too dated to revive — particularly on an executive committee agenda.

Time management

If a doctor–manager wishes to scrutinise the work pattern of others in the organisation, he must first put his/her own house in order. He/she, more than anyone else, must not waste time. Time is precious and is itself a limited resource.

In medicine there is usually a specific timetable of a number of fixed sessions per week. This should make it easy to allocate specific time for management, although planning ahead may be difficult in specialties where there is a large emergency element (General Medicine and Surgery) or where the ongoing, non-emergency workload is unpredictable (Obstetrics). Management time should be protected so that managerial discussion and decisions can be made without interruption. You have to work at this by deploying staff to cover certain clinical sessions.

Prioritising jobs

Some jobs are more important than others. The less important ones are often the easiest ones to do, the ones you are most familiar with. These have to be recognised and relegated to second place on your agenda. The difficult ones are those where a nettle has to be grasped: these are the problems which demand time and energy, preferably uninterrupted time so that you are not distracted from the main purpose, e.g. often a strategem has to be developed in order to carry the move through a committee stage. You should also differentiate urgent from important tasks: often the urgent ones are not important but they have to be dealt with quickly, otherwise they clog up your desk. You should be able to find some items which can be delegated.

It is worth doing a time-and-motion study on yourself at some stage, listing the daily or weekly events, including all the interruptions and noting all the work you have to take home and the time spent there in dealing with it. This will help in prioritising duties in the future.

Unscheduled interruptions

People cannot understand how disruptive these can be. If you operate an open-door policy where you are always accessible such interruptions are inevitable — a Clinical Director and Business Manager must hear the question 20 times a day: "Sorry to interrupt but can you spare a few minutes?" No progress can be made in planning major developments if you have to answer the telephone or change your train of thought every few minutes.

Having said that, and leaving aside medical emergencies, you should try to set aside some times in the week when you can (one way or another) make it clear that you do not wish to be disturbed, and (so as not to offend people) some other times when you are freely available for any discussion. In this respect it is important to have an office which can be used for informal meetings. There needs to be enough space for several people to sit comfortably around a (working) table.

'Uninterrupted windows', if you can find them, are a good time to sit back and get an overview of how the organisation is running. This should be 'creative-thinking' time, time spent on initiative rather than reactive work and it should include some appraisal of your own job and why you are doing it.

Information sources

As doctor–manager you will need to know how to access information. Most hospitals are now developing patient care information systems, some of which are very complex. However, the general trend is for them to be patient-based rather than administration tools.

In the past, computers were mainly used for management purposes, e.g. in areas such as finance, personnel and administration, but in the post-Griffiths' NHS, and particularly since the recent NHS reforms, it has been realised that information is not just an administrative control mechanism but a corporate resource and can be used in decision making and patient management. In fact, the present policy is to insist that information technology (IT) is 'person centred' (IM&T Strategy and Overview 1992).

Information should facilitate the work of decision makers and possession of information confers the ability to influence change (Hewett 1990).

- To be useful, information must be timely, accurate and comprehensive, so it should be gathered at the point of service.
- Large volumes of data are likely to be generated and so computer systems must be able to communicate effectively.
- Doctors will only collect information that they find useful. Therefore information must be patient centred with derived management information a by-product.

Five principles form the basis of the new Information Management and Technology (IM&T) strategy for the NHS (Information Management Group 1992, Leaning 1993):

- information should be person based;
- systems should be integrated;
- management information should be derived from operational clinical systems;

- data should be secure and confidential;
- data should be shared across the NHS.

The UK has a long history of collecting health service information but this has been mainly for administrative purposes. For example, the Hospital In-Patient Enquiry (1957) and Hospital Activity Analysis (1969) provided information for health care planners and providers. Defects became apparent over the years because information that was provided was limited in its usefulness (NAHAT NHS Handbook 1993).

In 1980, the Korner Steering Group on health service information was set up. The plan was that managerial information should be a by-product of operational systems and not a separate exercise, and that the information collected should be timely, accurate and relevant. The concept of a Minimum Data Set (MDS) was introduced which defined the basic information requirements for local management.

Health Service Indicators (previously Performance Indicators)

The Korner Steering Group identified sets of Health Service Indicators (HSI) which would enable DHAs to compare their activity with that of other districts in England. There are now about 2000 indicators and the package is issued free to all RHAs and DHAs. FHSA indicators are also used for the management of the Family Health Services. Recently, responsibility for HSIs has been transferred to the Finance and Corporate Information branch of the NHSME.

Information Management Group

The various groups dealing with information were brought together under the umbrella of the Information Management Group (IMG) of the NHSME. Recently, the IMG published *NHS Information Systems: Next Steps*, which focussed on the information issues associated with the internal market. In 1992, the NHS Information Management and Technology Strategy was launched by the IMG. The strategy's objective is to achieve a patient record that will be accessible whenever a patient is treated and to build on that record an entire clinical information system.

Central to this overall strategy is the ability to communicate information throughout the NHS. This is not yet possible but it is expected that ultimately each citizen will have a unique NHS number and that information will be available across the country to any clinician caring for a patient.

A prerequisite for such a standard is a shared language, a list of common terms capable of being coded and thus transmitted electronically (a thesaurus of clinical terms and groupings).

On the back of information collected for patient care will come aggregated information that can be used for resource management, budgeting, audit and research on outcomes. A number of facilitating projects are underway including:

- Hospital Information Support Systems (HISS) — remit is to explore the use of integrated information systems in large acute hospitals;
- Developing Information Systems for Purchasers (DISP) — has examined the business processes of DHAs and FHSAs as purchasers and is addressing the information requirements of GP fundholders and reviewing the implications of purchasing community care;
- Community Information for Providers (CISP) — aims to support the information and contracting needs of community providers.

Clinical coding

In 1990 the clinical coding system developed by James Read became Crown copyright. The aim is to develop Read codes so that they become the standard language of clinical terms used in health care throughout the NHS by April 1994. When finalised, the Read codes will be applied automatically by the software running the clinical information systems.

Health Care Resources Groups

Illnesses and treatments can be categorised, thereby allowing patient details to be presented in small groups. This should allow information to be assessed more easily, e.g. patterns of activity and resource implications.

Health Care Resource Groups (HRGs) describe episodes of inpatient care which have clinically similar diagnoses or procedures and which are grouped together according to typical resource consumption (measured in length of stay in bed days). HRG definitions are defined by panels of clinicians and are available on PC-based software which may also be incorporated into case-mix management systems. They work from the standard data set which hospitals already routinely collect. Because patient-specific data have been aggregated into typical groups, the case-mix is presented in a managable and understandable format (IMG report, Health Care Today 1993).

In order to communicate effectively between one clinician and another, one hospital and another, purchaser and provider, all parties should speak the same language. It is hoped that HRGs will provide an instantly applicable language. HRG software and definitions are released by the NHSME IMG and are issued free to NHS hospitals on request.

Contract Categories, a case-mix language for contracting, are currently being developed for HRGs. It is envisaged that there will be six to eight contract categories per main specialty and they are likely to be the basis of contracting for 1995/1996.

The overall plan is to develop a complete, standard language for health. HRGs are part of the complete thesaurus of coded clinical terms and groupings becoming available.

Patient Care Information Systems

The Patient Care Information System (PCIS) chosen by our Trust is a hospital-wide information system covering the two hospital sites which comprise the Trust. It uses a large computer to store and send information, automatically or at the request of users, to the people who need to act upon it. The computer adds (or should add) speed and accuracy to the collection and sharing of information and can perform many tasks such as sorting, copying, summarising, checking and retrieving information which would otherwise be done by people.

It is inappropriate in this book to describe in detail our PCIS system. Suffice it to say that its great advantage (over other similar systems) is that it has been designed to improve patient care via efficient communication rather than simply to be used as a tool for gathering management information. It has a number of disadvantages, the main ones being: it is a large and complex system which has already taken several years to install — some departments are still coming 'on-line'; the learning curve for users is long, which creates problems in the clinical arena where time is short (e.g. entering patients' details into the system during the course of an antenatal clinic — we have calculated that it takes a trained midwife 1 hour per patient to do this task!); it is a very expensive piece of equipment; and, of course, it has to be paid for by various cost-realisation programmes — staff find it hard to accept these when the benefits are slow to appear.

Our own view is that the system will eventually prove to be extremely valuable and better than 'stand-alone' computer systems which some hospitals and trusts have adopted.

Conflict with other interests

Service

A price you have to pay for adopting a managerial role is that you have less time to practice clinical medicine. You will have to delegate clinics, etc. If you have a skilled and supportive team of junior doctors this is more feasible. Alternatively, it may be possible, if resources allow it, to employ additional staff on a part-time basis.

Keeping up-to-date is an even more important consideration. There is a serious conflict between management duties and keeping up-to-date with service progress.

Example.

In the surgical specialties the current trend is towards minimally invasive surgery. There are new techniques available such as endometrial laser ablation and diathermy resection, laparoscopic cholecystectomy, hernia repair, etc., which need a completely new surgical approach to that provided by conventional teaching. This means that Consultants as well as juniors are having to learn a very different set of surgical rules, and this takes time.

Rightly or wrongly, the management issues usually assume priority because other peoples' interests are at stake (and for many projects you need them on your side). This is another dilemma you have to face: are you in the business for personal satisfaction or for the benefit of the team?

Teaching and learning

In most clinical specialties, teaching and clinical work are inseparable, therefore if clinical work is compromised, so is teaching. This includes the teaching of senior postgraduates, junior medical staff, undergraduates, nursing and paramedical staff.

The extent of consultant teaching and supervision of junior staff has received a lot of comment recently. In view of the increasing level of litigation consultants are being asked to spend more time supervising juniors. For the doctor–manager it is difficult to fit in *ad hoc* teaching sessions, teaching ward rounds, etc. Ward rounds, general clinics and subspecialty interest clinics have to be geared towards patient throughput and activity rather than teaching. The long-term effects of the drive towards service rather than teaching and research will have to be studied closely.

As doctor–manager you may also miss out on your own postgraduate development. The involvement with management work means that you can rarely attend hospital postgraduate teaching sessions (e.g. grand rounds). Some of these are important communication events as much as learning episodes. They are occasions when you can meet junior staff and hear their views on clinical and non-clinical topics.

In more general terms, emphasis is now on continuing medical education for senior staff. There was a time when a consultant surgeon could be kept up-to-date by the registrar: this is no longer the case. Surgery is changing so fast that senior staff themselves (in order to teach their juniors) are having to learn new techniques and new philosophies about surgical management. Senior consultants in surgery are not only at the start of a learning curve of new surgical techniques but also of increasing management responsibilities. The combination of the two may be too much for the individual.

Research

Clinical research needs thinking time in which there are no interruptions so it is an unrealistic undertaking for a doctor–manager. Furthermore, clinical cases, who may be the subjects of clinical research, may have to be seen, for example, pre- and post-operatively by junior staff who are not part of a research team and so close supervision of project work is not possible. Also, clinical research needs a full and dedicated team which is unlikely to be funded inside a DGH Trust.

This is unfortunate because research activity tends to take a hospital from a regular service unit (which may be very good) towards a unit which is a 'centre of excellence'. It is only through research papers and publications that the rest of the world knows how much you are achieving. This publicity generates interest amongst doctors who wish to work with you because it will further their careers. And so recruitment improves. The danger behind the high-throughput/low-cost philosophy is that it may destroy, or prevent the generation of, centres of excellence.

Personal life

Although two sessions per week may be considered enough for Clinical Directorate work it would be more realistic to say that you have to be prepared to devote *personal* time to doing the job, i.e. in the evenings and at weekends.

Personal career and development

A doctor who develops a special interest in, for example, Royal College activities, may be 'promoted' to senior rank within that organisation. The same may apply to BMA and Defence Society work, but for you as doctor–manager there is nothing at the end of your period of office unless you want to aim for a Chief Executive job — which would mean giving up clinical work entirely. Because of this and the long learning curve there is a tendency to stay in post as long as possible believing that it will be too difficult for someone else to pick up the threads. However, you should not lose sight of the other features of your job which may be suffering because of the time spent on management. Also, the intensity of work needed in the larger Directorates cannot be sustained for ever, and it is only fair to the organisation to allow new blood to be introduced after a time. We have already referred to the difficulties in ensuring a cascade of information downwards to junior and non-medical staff; senior staff can perhaps be best appraised of the new organisation by working in it more closely. So there is a case for every clinician doing a spell in the management arena. If everyone is aware of what is needed for the department to succeed, it should be possible for some of the work to be shared, and for the Clinical Director to delegate more easily.

Furthermore, different Clinical Directors have different approaches to management; some are more innovative than others. Reference has been made to the speed of change in the NHS; it is likely that at different stages and with the development of the new structures one type of leadership is more appropriate than another.

So, even though there is no promotion beyond the Clinical Directorship, you should probably relinquish the post after 3 years or so. From there on you can use your new leadership skills for the corporate good of the service and to further some other career aspect.

Summary

We have outlined the difficulties inherent in doctor–managing: in particular, the problems associated with 'managing' one's peers; the limited amount of business management training currently provided in a doctor's training; and the natural tendency for doctors to behave as individuals rather than as members of a team.

A description of a Clinical Director has been given, on the understanding that this will vary between directorates and hospitals. However, the principles that govern the success of a doctor–manager remain the same, the main criterion being leadership ability.

The long- and short-term problems that a doctor–manager faces have been described with emphasis being placed on proactive rather than reactive management.

There may be several different models in which a Clinical Directorate can function. We have described the genesis and development of the one with which we have become familiar. The importance of identifying clear terms of reference for each subgroup in the Directorate has been stressed, as well as lines of communication upwards and downwards in the organisation.

Clearly, teamwork is essential, particularly between the members of the DMT. There is a great deal of overlap of their duties, particularly those of the Business and Clinical Nurse (now Service) Managers.

The changing pattern of Directorate structure has been referred to briefly and is discussed further in Chapter 7.

It should be clear from the above account that being a doctor–manager or Clinical Director is not easy: it is hard work; time consuming; and there is little at the end of the job other than the satisfaction of seeing a job well done.

Further reading

Audit Commission
1992 Community Care: Managing the Cascade of Change. HMSO, London

Caring for People
1989 Community Care in the Next Decade and Beyond. White Paper, DHSS. HMSO, London

Chantler C
1989 How to do it. Be a manager. British Medical Journal 298: 1505–1508

Garratt S
1985 Manage your time. Fontana/Collins, London

Ham C, Merry P (eds)
National Association of Health Authorities and Trusts (NAHAT)
1993 NHS Handbook, 8th edn. JMH Publishing, Tunbridge Wells, Kent

Handy C B
1985 Understanding Organisations, 3rd edn. Penguin Books, Harmondsworth

Harvey-Jones J
1988 Making it Happen. Fontana/Collins, London

Health Services Information Steering Group
1980 A report on the collection and use of information about clinical activity in the NHS. HMSO, London (Korner report)

Hewett D J
1990 The age of information technology. Hospital Update April: 283–284

Hudson R
1993 Local authorities and community care. In Ham C, Merry P (eds) NAHAT NHS Handbook, 8th edn. JMH Publishing, Tunbridge Wells, Kent

Information Management and

Technology Group of the NHSME
1992 Getting better with information: IM&T Strategy overview. NHSME, London

Information Management Group, NHSME
1992 Getting Better with Information: Handbook for IM&T Specialists. NHSME, Leeds

Information Management Group Report
1993 Health Care Today 10: 19–21

Keen J, Malby R
1992 Nursing power and practice in the United Kingdom National Health Service. Journal of Advanced Nursing 17: 863–870

Kreitner R
1992 Management, 5th edn. Houghton Mifflin, Boston

Leaning M S
1993 The new information management and technology strategy of the NHS. British Medical Journal 307: 217

National Health Service and Community Care Act
1990. HMSO, London

Patients' Charter
1992 DoH. HMSO, London

Scrivens E
1988a Doctors and managers: never the twain shall meet? British Medical Journal 296: 1754–1755

Scrivens E
1988b The management of clinicians in the English National Health Service. Social Policy and Administration 22: 22–34

Stewart R
1989 Leading in the NHS. A Practical Guide. The MacMillan Press, London

Turrill E A
1986 Change and Innovation. A challenge for the NHS. The Institute of Health Services Management, London

Turrill E A
1993 Transforming Doctors Dilemmas. A management development manual for doctors and their managerial colleagues. Turrill Ltd

3 Managing resources

Introduction

Managing financial resources is a great challenge and can be very rewarding. Financial control of a budget equals the power to achieve change and this is what the doctor–manager is there to do.

It is likely that you will be a practising clinician (for whom management is only a part-time activity), so the quality of your support staff is vital. This is particularly true in budgetary management. You will be expected to take overall responsibility for the strategic planning of the service and the financial 'bottom line', but the day-to-day planning, allocation and management of resources will be performed by your support staff, namely your Business Manager, Clinical Nurse or Specialty Manager, and Financial Assistant (who may or may not be part of the Directorate team).

The interaction of the Directorate team is particularly important in the management of financial resources, as most of the Directorate's financial management will be delegated to senior managers, and there will be little time for you, as Clinical Director, to devote to the examination of the detailed expenditure. The team must have a clear understanding of the corporate financial goals, and an appreciation of the extent of flexibility that exists within the budget. It is essential that this is a trusting relationship as the capacity for pursuing an individual 'professional' agenda inevitably exists.

The budget

A budget is a plan quantified in monetary terms, prepared and approved prior to a defined period of time, showing planned income to be generated and expenditure to be incurred during that period and capital to be employed to attain a given objective.

The *functions* of a budget are shown in Table 3.1. A number of general points need to be made.

First, the budget must be agreed by all parties to be adequate for the task in hand. For many Units setting anything that resembles an accurate budget in a completely new format and structure is likely to cause

Budget is used to:

Plan	**Future activities**
Communicate	**Information plans**
Motivate	**People re activity**
Control	**Effectiveness and efficiency**

Table 3.1 The functions of a budget

significant problems, and the initial availability of accurate financial data may be extremely scarce. In such cases, some form of a 'trial' budgetary period should be assessed with revisions and adjustments being made at the end of the process. A poorly constructed budget, whether over- or under-funded, deflects from the real issues of managing the service — underfunding diverts energy and will cause disillusionment with the whole process: overfunding can lead to poorly managed and under-utilised resources.

Secondly, in dividing an entire hospital budget into service areas managed by Clinical Directors, the Chief Executive is relinquishing a significant part of control over the hospital 'bottom line'. The hospital, as a whole, is still subject to external financial pressures, e.g. cost improvement programmes, withdrawal of resources for GP fund-holders' budgets, etc. There must be some acknowledgement of a corporate responsibility (at Arrowe Park this is through the Hospital Council, see p. 31).

Example.

At the start of our Trust status a financial crisis revealed that the whole hospital was seriously overspent only 3 months into the financial year. Ten of the 13 Clinical Directorates had major projected overspends at year end even though their base budgets had only recently been agreed (our Directorate's budget was in balance and was projected to be so at year end). The dilemma for the Chief Executive was whether or not to expect the financially healthy Directorates to bail out the rest (by one means or another — and 'for the corporate good') or to abandon the failures. Clearly he could not do the latter, although revoking the recently agreed business plans of the healthy Directorates was against all basic principles of good management. Such situations put immense strain on the working partnership between the Clinical Director and the Chief Executive.

In this instance, the Chief Executive (who is charged with the responsibility of running a financially viable Trust) had to agree financial recovery plans with overspent Directorates, using a combination of 'carrot and stick' with underspent Directorates to maintain a financial status quo.

Budget setting and management

Zero-based budgeting is the ideal, i.e. X hysterectomies @ £X00 each will be performed in the forthcoming financial year and therefore £X000 is needed, but *incremental budgeting* is what really happens in the NHS (at least in our experience). An attempt is made to determine past outcomes in respect of revenue costs and adjustments are made for the forthcoming period. A base is established for the next budgetary period. Unfortunately, the limitations of the measurement of activity and the hospital information systems are likely to prevent an accurate connection being made between activity and resource allocation. Another danger with this system is that inefficiencies are perpetuated.

As mentioned above, the initial allocation of the budget to a Clinical Directorate may well contain inaccurate elements. In many cases it will represent the Finance Department's 'guesstimate' of the amount of money involved in operating various parts of the service; this is not necessarily the Finance Department's fault in as much as the global accounting system does not necessarily provide an easy facility for separating expenditure into Clinical Specialties — however, it does mean that a rigorous examination of the coding of all expenditure needs to take place in the first trial period of budget setting. Information systems, coding analyses and rigorous financial management go hand in hand in the first instance. In our experience after more than 4 years of Clinical Directorates and this length of experience in managing a budget, we find there are still inaccuracies surfacing from time to time. There has to be constant surveillance of coded expenditure.

Once a budget is set, agreed to be accurate and the Clinical Director is satisfied that the financial reports coming through do reflect valid financial activity, it is essential that systems are set up to monitor trends in the levels of expenditure against each heading. As in all budget management, it is necessary to identify irregular trends in expenditure before they become irreversible.

Hospitals vary in the scope of financial management and control that is delegated to Directorate level. In our Unit about 65% of total hospital revenue/expenditure is delegated to specialty level and includes:

- medical staff salaries;
- nursing staff salaries;
- administrative and clerical support staff salaries;
- drugs;
- medical and surgical supplies and equipment;
- printing and stationery.

Within these headings there is virtually complete discretion in terms of expenditure; changes in skill mix, increases/reductions in staff numbers, etc. Within the overall budget these are quite acceptable as long as the service quality is maintained and the overall budget balances. In our system any proposed radical changes do need some prior discussion with the Chief Executive, Finance Department and Chief Nurse.

Clinical Directors in other hospitals with resource management systems may not be so fortunate. For example, whilst the management of staff salaries may be delegated, any change in the grades or mix will be controlled by the Personnel Department or the Chief Nurse, thus severely limiting the flexibility allowed the Directorate.

This budget-setting exercise is a radical change from what preceded it in the NHS. It is almost inevitable that there will be considerable tension, even suspicion, between the Financial Director and his Department, and the Directorate's Management Team. For the system to succeed the Directorate Team has to prove capable of managing the budget effectively and the Finance Department has to provide timely, credible and reliable financial information from the Central Ledger System to support the coded expenditure of the Directorate.

The following are essentials for successful budget setting:

- be clear about workload; identify increasing trends and resource consequences;
- look at staff turnover, skill-mix and training needs;
- cost any developments;
- investigate 'disinvestment';
- estimate effects of external pressures;
- involve senior doctors and nurses in the process.

Involving other clinicians and senior nurse managers in the budget setting process has the benefit of raising awareness in terms of their own clinical practice and its effect on the financial resources available, and secondly, ties them in to a corporate responsibility for the use of the Directorate's resources.

> **Example.**
>
> A formal budget-setting exercise in one Directorate revealed that a consultant was planning to change the prosthesis he had used for many years for one which had much superior clinical results, but which cost twice the price. On clinical grounds it was agreed that the new prosthesis should be adopted, but a similar resource saving had to be identified in order to cover what would have shown as an overspend on the Directorate's budget.

Accountability

As doctor–manager in a Clinical Directorate model, you will be expected to accept the responsibility and accountability for a global budget with which to run the specialty. The extent of budgetary functions devolved will obviously vary from hospital to hospital but it is likely that about 75% of the budget will be accounted for in staff salaries. In return for the money allocated to the specialty you are likely to have a 'contract' with the Chief Executive to agree to deliver on specific targets, e.g. to return a balanced budget at the end of the year, guarantee that a specified amount of activity will occur within that budget and that certain quality targets will be achieved.

Depending on the support that is available it may be that each budgetary heading is given to an individual to validate and manage as part of the Directorate team, or it may be that your Business Manager has the responsibility for validating the budget and line managers proceed to manage as part of their normal responsibilities. Whichever way is chosen, it is crucial that everyone is confident that financial statements represent an accurate report of expenditure.

Information

A robust financial monitoring system is an essential tool for effective Directorate management of resources. There is no single 'right' or prescriptive means of achieving this and the doctor–manager will be heavily dependent upon the Finance Department and its capacity to disaggregate costing information and coded expenditure back to the Directorate.

It is usual for all financial transactions, orders, purchases, etc., to be allocated a 'cost centre' code, which is an individual numerical identifier for the source of that expenditure. From this information it is possible to build up expenditure profiles against an allocated budget.

In our Directorate, a monthly expenditure summary is supplied by the Finance Department showing expenditure against budget for the month, and also cumulative figures broken down by budgetary heading. With this basic information the Business Manager is able to keep a trend analysis of each heading predicting outturn and investigating variances. More detailed information can be made available if required (e.g. if an unpredicted variance occurs) either from the ledger system, or from stand alone systems (e.g. pharmacy), where expenditure can be identified item by item.

When statements are validated by the Business Manager, they are discussed on a monthly basis by the Directorate as a group, highlighting issues which appear as a cause for concern.

Some examples where close scrutiny of the budget revealed irregularities are described below:

- Examination of the topping-up system on the wards revealed that £14 000 had gone adrift (possibly through wrong coding) on maternity pads!
- Investing in an IKON pregnancy kit on a gynaecology ward obviated the need (for those patients with irregular bleeding in possible early pregnancy) for hospitalisation (usually at weekends) whilst waiting for non-emergency pathology testing, thereby saving on bed usage.
- It was found that overtime done in other parts of the hospital by part-time gynaecology staff was being charged to our Directorate — to the tune of £6000 pa.

Staff involvement

Within the whole Directorate itself, responsibility for budgetary management should be devolved to the lowest possible level of accountability (a) to motivate staff to improve this aspect of management, and (b) to improve their individual skills and enhance team building.

The theoretical advantages of involving all levels of staff in exercises like this can be summarised as follows:

- the individual's knowledge and experience is expanded and initiative is encouraged;
- involvement in the planning process boosts morale;
- interprofessional and interdepartmental cooperation is enhanced;
- low-level managers become familiar with policies;

- targets set by the budget are more likely to be accepted;
- staff know where they fit in the department or specialty.

Motivating staff in these ways sounds easy, but takes time and energy.

Virement

Virement is the authorised transfer of funds from one budgetary heading to another.

The extent of virement within your budget (under the hospital's financial regulations), is likely to be a measure of the confidence of the Chief Executive's team in the abilities of the Directorate to manage responsibly. At its most complementary, you will be given the freedom for total virement between staff and non-staff, capital and revenue budgets — although in the early stages the Financial Director is likely to need a degree of control of virement between budget headings.

The degree to which budgetary manipulation is allowed will also depend on the Finance Director's view and assessment of the system — and of his/her own ability to participate in the change process. In our Directorate, for example, we have no capital budget; other hospitals do not allow virement between staff and non-staff budgets; others allow *no* change in staff grading other than that sanctioned centrally. As doctor–manager you should insist upon maximum flexibility of budgetary control within your department.

At the outset, it is vital that there is clear understanding between the Chief Executive, his/her team and yourself about the way that underspends and overspends at the end of any financial year are to be managed. The motivating factors in managing a budget are that any underspends, fortuitous or managed, can be reinvested in the Directorate. Without this agreement much of the incentive to invest time and effort into budgetary management disappears (the reader will note the contradiction between this and the example quoted on p. 66).

> **Example.**
>
> The reappraisal of drug usage in a Surgical Directorate freed up money to provide improved facilities for junior doctors — a dictation/study room. The provision of such a facility would not have been possible from any other source.

Given that any money realised will be reinvested directly into that clinical area is a great incentive for all staff within the Directorate to look carefully at practices which consume resources. Changes in practice will be easier to accept (e.g. the implementation of a drugs policy), if money is released to buy, for example, equipment on the wards. Perhaps it should be noted that NHS staff have become hardened and sceptical over the years, after a succession of cost improvement programmes, and it will be necessary for you to *prove* that their efforts produce a tangible benefit or result.

> Example.
>
> Our Directorate bought a modem fetal monitor for the antenatal unit using money raised from private patient charges. Because private patient money was used specifically in the Directorate in which it was raised, nursing staff could see how useful this resource is. In this instance it has had the effect of making midwives more receptive to amenity and private patients than before.

Role of the doctor–manager

Budget

Whilst accepting that the close scrutiny and day-to-day supervision of the budget is undertaken largely by the Business Manager and/or Financial Adviser, as doctor–manager you must have an overview of how the budget stands. You need to understand the broad principles of budgetary control; and to know the flexibility available in your Directorate's budget to allow you to make activity/service decisions.

First, you should have some vision of the future: this has been described in Chapter 2. The short-term business planning objectives itemised there can be extrapolated to the future; for example, what services should you be providing in 5 or 10 years' time? What critical external events may happen in the next 5 or 10 years and how do you make the most of any opportunities that arise? How do you change for the better and to meet different needs of the population?

Clearly, the Directorate's 'core mission' has to be married to the resources available: it may not be possible to do all of it at once — there may need to be a mid-point objective. However, you should not lose sight of the overall core mission when negotiating a budget for the next financial year or when presenting a business plan for the next period (e.g. 1-year or 5-year plan).

It has been recognised in our Directorate that there is a need for a teaching strategy. This will need money and a well-reasoned argument will have to be presented to the Chief Executive and to the purchasing bodies to provide additional money for teaching (and possibly research). This will be a hard task because the overriding consideration in the NHS reforms is service levels and quality. It may be some time before the influence of teaching and research on the quality of service is recognised.

Leaving these altruistic concerns aside, there are three elements in controlling budgets where you should lead.

1. REVIEW An ongoing review of expenditure — measuring actual expenditure against expected or anticipated budgetary provision.
2. REACT Investigating any variances:

   - establish the cause of budgetary variances;
   - involve the key staff in the process.

   Decide on the action to be taken (having considered options and the effect of that action on other parts of the service).
3. REVISE It is important to remember that a budget is not a static fixed item and the most effective and creative Clinical Directors will undertake a constant review of budgetary performance in order to allow them the flexibility to make service decisions.

Budget and activity

The control loop whereby budget and activity are compared is represented in Figure 3.1.

Service/activity decisions

Knowledge of the resource available within the budget and its flexibility will help you to manage both the internal and external environments affecting your Directorate. A useful way of looking at these environments is by one or more closed-loop systems, where error messages are identified and the error(s) corrected (Fig. 3.2).

Management of the internal environment is almost synonymous with resource management. You should have identified expenditure needed for this activity during the budget-setting exercise or be able to vire money from one heading to another according to priority.

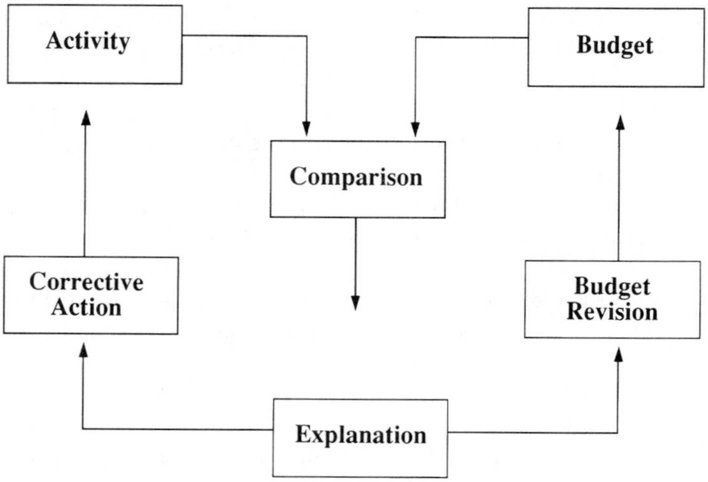

Figure 3.1 Control loop comparing budget and activity

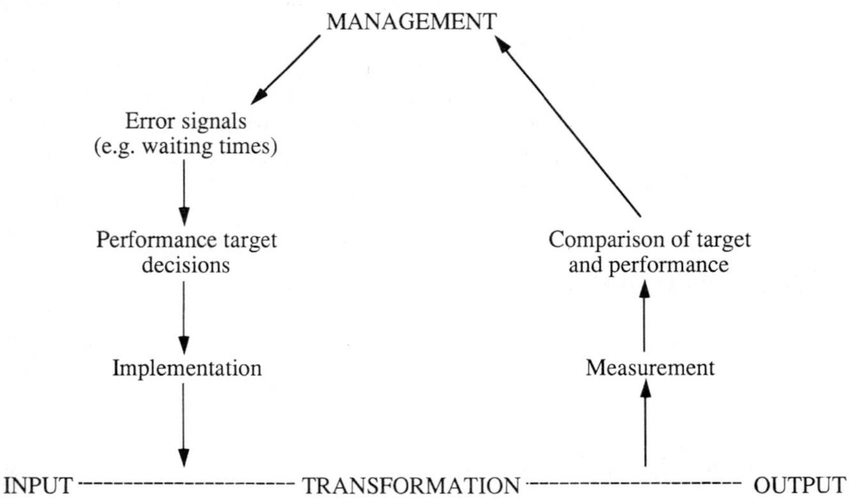

Figure 3.2 Service/activity. An internal closed-loop system

The performance target decisions in this example (Fig. 3.2) could be a new appointment system or taking on extra staff for an outpatient clinic. This decision has then to be implemented (by managing resources) and the effect on throughput of outpatients measured by comparing target and actual performance.

Example.

Until a short time ago patients referred to our Unit were having to wait an average of 52 weeks for an appointment. This state of affairs existed because of inertia in the system: there was no mechanism for dealing with it. Each consultant was working flat-out during clinic time; seeing as many 'add-on' patients as possible; but there was no effect on the clinic waiting time. With the flexibility of virement money it was possible to employ sessional staff to take on extra clinics (with some help from waiting list-initiative bids). Discourse with GPs has set guidelines for professional treatment and follow-up so that there are fewer unnecessary clinic visits; the appointment of a Staff Grace doctor has reduced the clinical load of the consultants and allowed tired junior staff time off after busy nights on call. The waiting time for an outpatient appointment is now a maximum of 10 weeks.

Other approaches to the problem can be constructed; e.g. the view of management by a member of the Board of Directors of a private company might be much more entrepreneurial and outward-looking. That approach would be to react to external pressures rather than internal ones (Fig. 3.3). To manage in this way, you may have to look for funds other than those in your set budget, or ensure that your business plan for the next year includes this item.

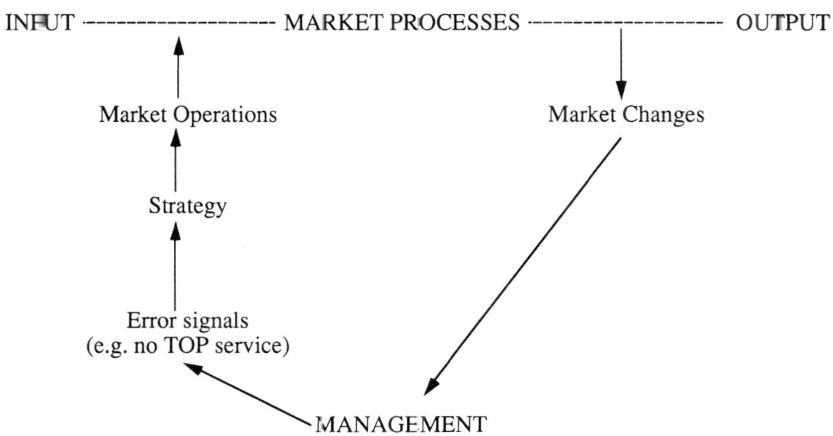

Figure 3.3 External pressures: overall progress measured against criteria

Example.

Within our own Directorate we were conscious of external demands for a better pregnancy counselling service, including pregnancy termination. Only a limited service was provided within our hospital. There were early referral schemes in the nearby city which seemed often to break down. For one reason or another patients were arriving at the hospital requesting termination at a late stage of pregnancy. We were distressed by this (particularly the junior doctors and the gynaecology nurses who were expected to deal with these cases and increasingly more of them refused to participate); GPs were annoyed because they were on the front line, so to speak, and were having to field the complaints from the public; worst of all, patients were sometimes having to endure the trauma of late termination when, had they been counselled earlier, the treatment might have been easier.

We agreed that a better service was needed. We negotiated a contract to provide the service with the fundholders (in this case the consortium representing the District's GPs) and the programme is now up and running. Patients are referred early; the programme includes detailed counselling, microbiological screening and post-operative advice; it is discrete and no longer invades the regular hospital activity. It is an excellent programme and had been welcomed with great enthusiasm by all parties.

In fact, in this instance we priced the implementation and first year's costs of the programme realistically and competitively but nevertheless were not fully funded by the purchasing consortium. We were under intense pressure from GPs to start the service (they already had wind of it), and from the Chief Executive. We could not refuse. In the next financial year we must negotiate (less naively) a better contract.

Example.

There is a groundswell of public opinion in favour of managing low-risk pregnancies more conservatively than before, i.e. there is a wish to move away from the high-tech supervision of labour which has been promoted during the last 20 years. Those of us who have lived throughout these times have seen what advantages technology can bring to reducing the risks of childbirth for both mother and baby. Nonetheless, a response has to be made to this external pressure and so we (as are other maternity units) are attempting to identify low-risk pregnancies which can be managed almost entirely by midwives and GPs. A review of the external environment has caused us to rethink our stance on the management of low-risk pregnancy. Clearly this has to be done without jeopardising the outcome for mother or baby, and sufficient safeguards have to be built into the system, but we have implemented team midwifery, so that there is more continuity of care for mother and baby; we have implemented a screening system for high-risk cases (which will have more Consultant time devoted to them); and identified low-risk pregnancies for midwife/GP care. One of the outcomes is to utilise midwives' skills more than has been possible in the recent past.

Resources being as limited as they are in the NHS, more effort has to be devoted to *resource management* and improving the efficiency of the internal system rather than *resource allocation*. Nevertheless, the function of the Directorate, in our view, is to look both inward to improve internal efficiency and outward to observe and respond to external pressures. In practice, a mixture of loop systems exists (Fig. 3.4).

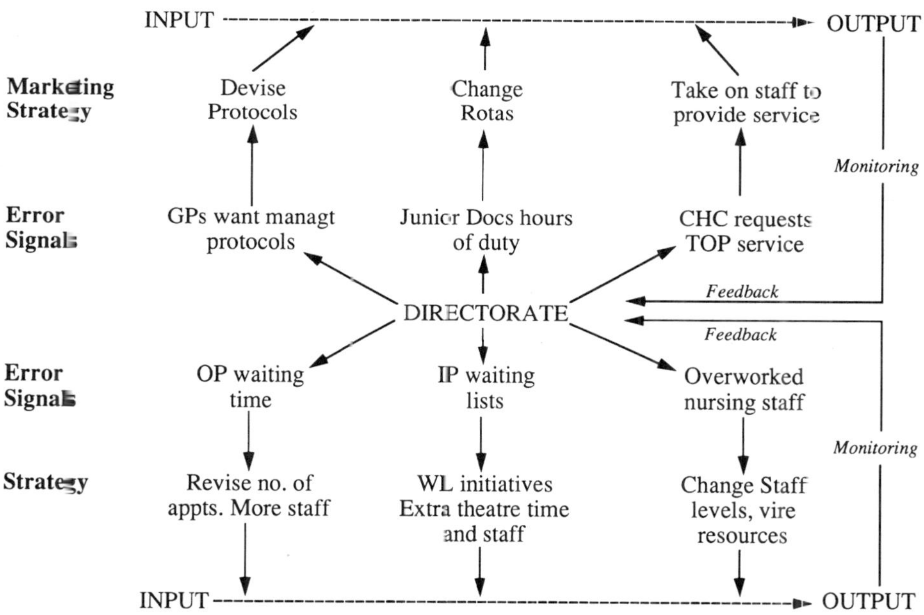

Figure 3.4 Environmental pressures, internal and external

In summary, as doctor–manager you must look outwards from the organisation because the success of various exercises will depend on an understanding of environmental demands and an ability to translate these into realisable objectives and strategies. Internally, you must organise and coordinate the activities of your Directorate, direct and control resources, monitor the performance of the system in relation to set objectives and criteria and take any remedial action necessary to improve efficiency. In the context of resource management these functions have to be undertaken as economically as possible.

The business plan

The NHS Management Executive now issues comprehensive guidelines about the production of business plans, particularly with reference to hospitals of Trust status. Whole hospital business plans are subject to a rigorous predetermined planning cycle, and Specialty/Directorate plans are likely to be required to dovetail into that timetable.

When devising a business plan and setting the strategic direction of the service, it is essential that this is done in the broader context of the service. National priorities as well as Regional and local priorities have to be addressed, as well as the corporate plans of the Trust within which your Directorate operates.

Purchasers will regard more favourably those services which appear to be addressing their priorities and targets — being 'tuned in' to these is essential for the appropriate development of the service.

> **Example.**
>
> A local hospital felt fortunate to recruit a consultant who specialised in vitreoretinopathy and invested heavily in the capital equipment necessary to enable him to begin to develop this service locally. At the same time the Regional SubCommittee was advising purchasers to centralise the service at the teaching hospital and 'disinvest' in procedures performed elsewhere.

Before you begin to construct your business plan you need:

- A statement of your core mission, i.e. your Directorate's long-term goals.
- A status review, i.e. an assessment of the strengths and weaknesses of your service relative to other units (a market research study) and an identification of the opportunities and the threats posed by those units and other influences.
- Plans for future services; e.g. your expectation of changes in the patterns of demand for your services over the next 3–5 years, including an assessment of the impact of changes on the way those services are delivered.
- Resources required to provide the above.
- The hospital's or Trust's corporate objectives against which you can match your own. For example, the Trust is likely to have itemised objectives under headings such as:

— contractual obligations;

— financial targets;

— quality issues;

— operational issues;

— human resource issues.

You can use this as a skeleton upon which to construct your own business plan. An example of the corporate objectives for 1 year in a Directorate is given in the Appendix at the end of this chapter. You may find this useful in building your own business plan.

The business plan itself does not have to be a single document. In the first year of production, our O&G Business Plan consisted of a profile of the objectives of the Directorate (see Appendix), a manpower statement, and a financial profile produced by the Business Manager.

Objectives

You will have a number of ***key objectives*** which are concise and challenging yet capable of being achieved and which are measurable. These will include objectives like implementing audit, meeting Patients' Charter obligations and service developments.

The ***action*** required to meet these objectives can be described, e.g. with regard to waiting times and waiting lists, you will need to study ***projected activity levels*** and anticipate ***targets*** and how they will be achieved.

Some objectives will have a ***quality element*** led by the Patients' Charter requirements and quality initiatives detailed by purchasing authorities.

Manpower analysis

A manpower analysis considers:

- ***Manpower and staff turnover.*** Current and future manpower requirements necessary to support the Directorate objectives, vacancy controls, sickness and absence rates, extended periods of leave, changeover of junior doctors, locum requirements, etc.
- ***Recruitment.*** Effects of poor recruitment in medical and nursing staff in relation to a key objective and solving any potential shortfall (by waiting list initiative funding, etc.).

- Opportunities for changes in ***skill mix*** and working practices.
- ***Training.*** Enrolled nurse conversion post basic courses, junior doctor training requirements.

Given the previously noted proportion of expenditure invested in staffing (75%), this exercise is worth devoting time to — miscalculations would seriously distort the financial outturn of the Directorate.

Financial profile

The financial profile has to be produced in the light of the financial position of the hospital as a Unit and to reflect realistically the resources likely to be available. The accountants within the hospital will be assessing fixed and variable, direct and indirect costs relating to the service provided by the Directorate, on a specialty basis and it is useful for the doctor–manager to have an appreciation of this cost structure for his/her area (Fig. 3.5).

The benefit of this type of analysis is to enable the doctor–manager to identify a break-even point. By plotting the combined cost curve against the prices charged, the financial optimum volume of activity emerges

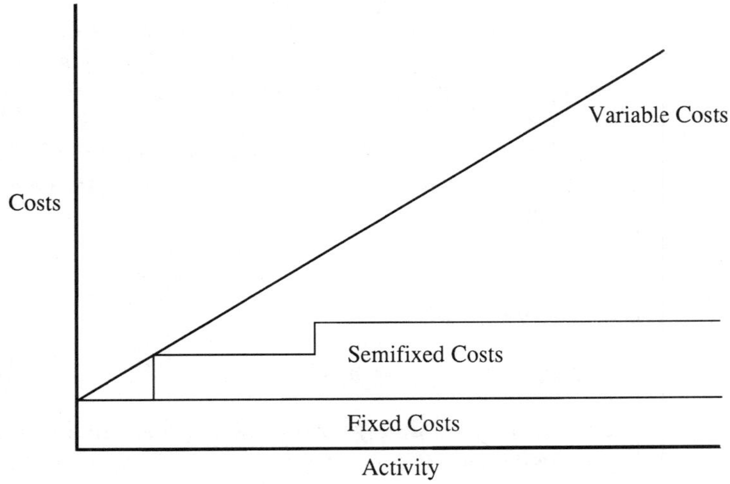

Where fixed costs = e.g. building, equipment overheads.
Semifixed = e.g. staff
Variables = e.g. consumables

Figure 3.5 Cost curves

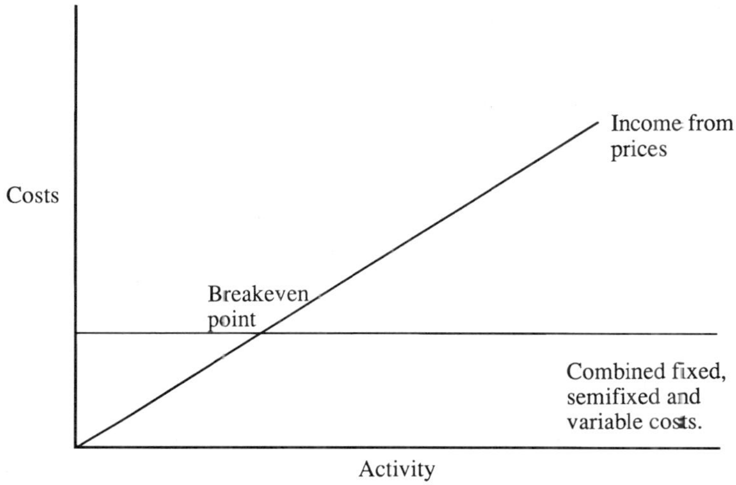

Figure 3.6 Break-even point

(Fig. 3.6). This exercise is essential when attempting to calculate spare capacity in the Unit and the level of marginal costs for additional activity (e.g. pricing waiting list initiative activity, etc.).

Much of this work is likely to be innovative whilst hospital costing procedures are increasing in sophistication; however, it is a valuable planning tool and helps the doctor–manager understand the financial performance of the Directorate.

In addition, the financial component of the business plan needs to include financial projections, detailing revenue requirements of service developments and rationalisation, historic trends in expenditure and forecast trends. There should be some indication also of capital requirements for replacement and new equipment, together with any specific proposals for alterations to existing buildings, etc.

Benefits

The potential benefits of a good business plan, over and above clarity on services, standards and resources, may be described as follows:

- ***Common purpose.*** The business plan is a powerful means of ensuring that different groups/disciplines in the organisation are 'signed up' to a common agenda.
- ***Communication.*** The business plan provides an effective means of

communicating with staff, the purchaser, the GPs and with the public.

- ***Decision making framework***. The business plan forces the Directorate to choose between competing options, to make decisions and, in addition, to demonstrate the implications of those decisions.
- It provides a ***plan for action*** and for the achievement of objectives within a given timescale.
- It gives a framework for ***using resources effectively***.
- It provides a means of ***monitoring performance against expectations***.

This is an area where you, as doctor–manager or Clinical Director, will take a strategic coordinating role, relying on the support staff to provide the detailed background work. Additionally, the business planning process is the means by which organisations translate their purpose and objectives into quantified plans to be used over a period of several years. As Clinical Directors tend to be appointed for a 3-year term of office, and for the reasons outlined above, it seems reasonable that the Directorate should produce some form of strategic plan for the service over, say, 5 years, and in line with the overall hospital direction and objectives. Indeed, it could well be a requirement of the Chief Executive that such a plan is produced. The business plan, at a basic level, should consist of a description of what the Directorate intends to do in terms of activity, what standard of service will be offered. This will be accompanied by an assessment of the financial and other resources required to achieve this, and ideally will be relative to other units in terms of range, quality and price of the service.

Problems

In the production of a business plan for the specialty and in the business planning process two elements are likely to prove particularly problematical.

First, the process itself is new to the NHS and, if handled insensitively, may confirm people's worst fears about the direction in which the NHS is moving. In particular, to run an effective unit, difficult decisions sometimes have to be made, e.g. Is there value in continuing to provide what may be an inferior clinical service in an area in which neighbouring units (hospitals) may excel? Does a choice have to be made between providing an average service on all fronts or an excellent service in limited subspecialties? The answers to these questions may well depend on the strength of the Clinical Director and the participation of clinical colleagues.

The other intensely problematical area is that of attempting to forecast income over a given period, at a time when GP fundholders are having a significant impact on the referral of work to any individual unit and purchasing authorities are experimenting with their new powers to purchase activity on the basis of cost and quality. However, even with these provisos, a well-constructed plan gives a clarity of purpose to any unit.

Contracting

Implementing the NHS reforms involved a massive analysis of resources which were to be allocated to individual purchasers to enable them to fund services for their resident population — this original 'quantum' exercise was based on historic expenditure by hospitals, taking no account of enormous variations in the cost of providing similar services. Very crudely, the implications of this are that hospitals which were cost efficient in 1990 have been left with little scope for improvement in subsequent contracting rounds, whereas those cost 'inefficient' units have more room for manoeuvre in changing practice, rationalisation of services and staffing and so can produce lower costs.

Because one of the principal themes of the reforms was the claim that 'money will follow the patient', it was anticipated that low-cost hospitals would attract more business and therefore flourish. This premise has proved to be somewhat fallacious (in hospitals outside London) in that any patient transfers which have taken place have usually been at the margins of clinical activity, e.g. small blocks of long waiters for hip replacements, cataracts, etc., or in funding extra contractual referrals (which probably account for less than 1% of the District budget).

The notion of 'contestability' is developing in many Districts, where detailed service specifications are drawn up for particular specialties where a problem may exist (e.g. long waiting times, high unit costs, unsatisfactory outcomes) and local provider units are invited to tender to provide the service. By and large this process, whilst potentially redefining service provision, will not seriously threaten the local hospital's viability — it is in the interests of purchasers to have a thriving local DGH — and the process will be used to attempt to lower costs, improve quality and generally 'sort out' service provision which is out of line with acceptable standards.

Contract monitoring

Within a Directorate it is vital that there are mechanisms for monitoring performance against individual and block contracts placed with the specialty. It is equally important to have intelligence about the perception of the performance of your specialty, both locally and regionally (performance relates to levels of activity and quality of service). The best way of achieving this is to hold regular contract reviews with your main purchasers, the most accessible of these will be the GP fundholders and it is likely that they will possess the most relevant information about performance. Whilst there may be a tendency for colleagues to question, or even discredit, this level of feedback, it is vital that criticisms, requirements and observations of your service are taken seriously and acted upon.

Performance measures

Most clinicians will be aware of the nationally-produced health service Performance Indicators (PIs). These indicators have been perceived to be a very crude comparison of measures of performance such as length of stay, theatre episodes, demand/provision of treatment, analysing patient demand by age group, resource/manpower investment for the provision of those services, number of consultants per head of population. The indicators are produced by an analysis of Korner returns at the end of each financial year and relate to a period 2 years previously. Whilst many anomalies can be exposed (e.g. excessively high gynaecology unit costs as a result of all medical staff who are obstetrics and gynaecology being assigned to the gynaecology cost heading), these indicators are being used as one of the elements of information for decision making at a purchasing consortium level. At almost every level in the NHS more attention is being paid to the quality and scope of recording the data. It is inevitable, therefore, that you will be drawn into this function.

It is clear from the evidence accumulated thus far that:

- No one PI should be taken alone — a number of indicators should be sought and a broad profile obtained.
- PIs depend on the denominator used and statistics have a history of being used and abused accordingly.
- PIs have never really been able to provide a valid and reliable answer to all potential relevant questions — but they do provide a series of clues as to what is or is not happening.

- The most fundamental flaw in using PIs in a comparative way is that the data are 2 years old. It must be obvious in all units that practice is changing so rapidly that 2 year old data do not, in any sense, provide an accurate representation of current efficiencies.

Benchmarking

Some commercial companies are offering an up-to-date service which analyses current hospital information and compares this with anonymised data from a pre-chosen set of 'peer group' hospitals. This allows hospitals to establish their competitiveness in terms of lengths of stay, throughput, etc., against other units of comparable size/population structure. This is a persuasive tool for internal change and is powerful in terms of negotiation with purchasers.

It is likely that purchasers will develop (or may already have developed) this analytical capacity for their own provider units — it remains to be seen how quickly a national system for current information comparison will develop.

Raising revenue

Cost improvement programmes

Most clinicians will be familiar with the yearly round of cost improvements, as another way of raising 'revenue' to fund hospital services. Cost Improvement Programmes (CIPs) have been set at circa 1% for the past years and are likely to remain at this level for the forseeable future. The definition of cash releasing cost improvement is very specific — it is an improvement in the use of resources by reducing the costs of running the service whilst simultaneously achieving the same or an increased level of output.

In our Unit, in the initial years of clinically managed budgets, CIP targets were not passed on to Directorates, and were absorbed by the central management functions. However, as Directorates account for 65% of the hospital expenditure, tackling CIP has now to be faced at specialty level. The Chief Executive has allowed individual Directorates the discretion to determine how and where the money is raised, and the yearly CIP has to be addressed alongside all the other calls on the Directorate resources.

Income generation

In recent years, income generation has featured increasingly on the management agenda. National targets for income generation are set at around £80m each year, and each hospital is likely to have a designated 'Income Generation Officer' with this responsibility.

An important aspect of income generation is the Health and Medicines Act (1988) which gives DHAs additional powers to raise income. The powers consist of:

- acquiring, producing, manufacturing and supplying goods;
- acquiring land;
- supplying accommodation;
- providing instruction;
- exploiting and developing ideas;
- applying commercial charges.

At specialty level the potential for generating income is more limited than for the hospital as a whole. However, new money is a welcome addition to departmental funds and the following list represents some of the initiatives our Directorate has implemented to generate around £30 000 each year:

- sponsorship of appointment cards and other specialty literature;
- organisation of specialty courses;
- charity appeals, sponsored activities;
- lease of space in the antenatal clinic to Mothercare for a shoplet;
- percentage of sales on certain specialty related objects, e.g. commemorative birth plates;
- advertising;
- marketing amenity facilities.

Summary

Managing resources is one of your most fundamantal responsibilities as doctor–manager, although it is important to recognise that your success in budgetary management will depend largely on the expertise of your support managers, in particular the Business Manager.

We have described what a budget is, and how it should be managed using the *review*, *react* and *revise* principles. Business tools for assisting service decisions have been described with the encouragement to look not only at the internal environmental pressures, but also at external pressures with some degree of entrepreneurialism.

The benefits of writing a good business plan have been listed, attention being drawn to its function as a decision-making framework and plan for action. It is a powerful means of ensuring that everybody in the organisation is 'signed up' to a common agenda.

Further reading

Appleby J
1993 Financing the NHS. In: Ham C, Merry P (eds) NAHAT NHS Handbook, 8th edn. JMH Publishing, Tunbridge Wells, Kent, pp. 45–54

Health and Medicines Act 1988. HMSO, London

Hunter D (ed)
National Association of Health Authorities and Trusts 1993 Rationing Dilemmas in Health Care, Research Paper No. 8. NAHAT, London

APPENDIX: EXAMPLE OF A BUSINESS PLAN

Key result area	Objective
SERVICE MANAGEMENT	• Constitute single/cohesive O & G Directorate
CONTRACTUAL OBLIGATIONS	• Achieve agreed activity targets • Achieve agreed quality targets • Reduce length of stay
MEET FINANCIAL TARGETS	• Return balanced budget • Attract external income to Directorate • Capital programme
QUALITY ISSUES	Achieve agreed quality targets

Action

- Establish lines of decision making/responsibility and communication within medical, nursing and managerial arenas across the two halves of the Directorate
- Solve inter-relationship issues
- Establish a managerial structure for the new subspecialty outpatient unit

Gynaecology

- Personal care plans
- Agree common policies regarding patient discharge
- Increase day case work to 45%
- Work up proposal for day case termination service

Obstetrics

- Reduce antenatal stay. Identify need for and work up proposal for antenatal assessment unit
- Reduce postnatal stay to 2.5 days. Earlier discharge for primigravidae and multigravidae

- Extend income generating initiatives (in Obstetrics, Mothercare, appointment cards sponsorship, etc.)
  Target £25 000
- Improve private patient facilities in Gynaecology: upgrade siderooms, install TVs, telephones

Gynaecology

Establish self-contained Gynaecology Outpatient Department comprising:

- Further development of subspecialty services in Urodynamics, Colposcopy/Laser treatment, Infertility
- Improvements to environment of gynaecology outpatient facility
- Establish outpatient minor procedure area

Maternity

- Explore funding for Clinic Creche
- Develop ward for use as antenatal assessment clinic

- Prenatal diagnostic service (e.g. screening all women for Down's Syndrome)
- Antenatal Clinic:
  (i) Refurbish Antenatal Clinic (outer area)
  (ii) Create plans for inner area refurbishment
  (iii) Explore alternatives for securing funding for Clinic Creche
- Create corporate identity for midwifery unit with staff uniforms, display areas

APPENDIX: (*Cont*)

Key result area	Objective
ORGANIZATIONAL DEVELOPMENTS *CLINICAL*	• Ongoing commitment to shift towards minimally invasive surgery for some gynaecological disorders
NURSING STAFF	Maximise role of Midwife and extend role of Gynaecology Nurse
CONSULTANT STAFF	Achieve balance of subspecialty expertise across Unit
JUNIOR STAFF	• Achieve national recommenced hours of work • Expand subspecialty expertise

Action

- Continued quality issues with establishment of quality circles
- Action on midwifery monitor
- Extend Health Education Initiatives, detailed programme to be available by October
- Environmental improvements on Gynaecological Wards. Improve side room accommodation
- Implement family centred care
- Ongoing monitoring of quality of service by monthly audit, PNM
- Display within Directorate deficiencies in care, e.g. complaints, medicolegal cases, etc.
- Conduct environmental survey in Maternity Unit

With funding from Waiting List Initiative:

- Develop endometrial laser ablation, endometrial diathermy resection as alternatives to hysterectomy
- Expand use of laparoscopic endoscopy and laser and diathermy treatment of endometriosis, ovarian cysts, etc.
- Develop use of day case facilities including day case theatre for laparoscopic surgery, tubal occlusions, etc.
- Establish outpatient facility for hysteroscopy, endometrial sampling, etc.
- Establish outpatient cystoscopy service
- Cost out early termination unit

- Midwifery involvement in Drugs Service
- Midwifery Management System
- Midwifery Care Plans
- Extend work of Joint Breast Initiative
- Implement Midwifery Standards
- Extend role of Gynaecology Nurse, e.g. smears, minor procedures, infertility investigation, urodynamic investigation, etc.

- Appoint replacement consultant, bearing in mind service needs and community pressures
- Investigate possibility of creating new consultant post in O&G from 'new consultant' monies from DOH
- Encourage/support via Consortium for the General Surgeons' bid for a Consultant Urologist. Appraise purchasing consortium of value of such a post to complement urogynaecology special interest

- Reduce junior doctors' hours in line with national and RCOG guidelines. Establish new rota system to allow time off after full night on labour ward duty
- Appoint Staff Grade Doctor

APPENDIX: (*Cont*)

Key result area	Objective
CLINICAL RESEARCH & DEVELOPMENT	Increase academic/clinical development profile
	• Increase academic/clinical development profile • Accelerate trend towards assisted conception by IVF
	• Influence purchaser priorities for development
COMMUNICATION	• Improve lines of communication with GPs, CHC, etc. to allow stronger consumer voice in the direction of service

Action

- Investigate possibility of creating post of Associate Specialist to co-ordinate colposcopy/cervical cytology services
- Investigate feasibility of securing research for infertility work, to be funded by industry
- Submit protocol for pelvic floor research project to fund research registrar in urogynaecology

- Expand session for urodynamic testing to reduce waiting time for investigation. Explore possibilities of securing funding for extra technical staff
- Appraise purchasers of need for Sphincter Centre for treatment of intractable incontinence
- Establish Sphincter Centre
- Secure funding for same
- Enlist help from AMS for theatre staff training, GP seminars, etc.
- Continue research programme into prosthetic surgery
- Continue research into the aetiology of detrusor instability
- Establish Structure of Infertility Unit (i.e. coordinating nurse, etc.)

- Encourage cooperation between NHS and private sector (using embryologist across sites). Develop transport IVF
- Consider feasibility of employing embryologist
- Establish outpatient area for ultrasound examination, egg retrieval, etc. (instead of using inpatient beds)
- Establish Preconception Clinic

- Sphincter Centre and funding of sphincter programme
- Increased funding for Urogynaecology Unit to £40 000
- Equipment funding for urogynaecology, theatres, day case unit, antenatal clinic, antenatal wards
- Target £150 000

- GP seminars, open days, etc. 3 per year
- Establish separate Maternity case sheets
- Replace cooperation cards with hard backed folder enclosing current computer printout of antenatal records
- Develop patient held notes

4 Audit

Introduction

We may now be on the threshold of a third revolution of medical care. The first was the rapid expansion of scientific medicine and hospital technology, the second was the era of cost containment. The third will be the era of assessment and accountability. In order to provide a basis for decisions on the future funding and organisation of health care, we have to know more about relative costs, safety and effectiveness of all that doctors do during the diagnosis, treatment and prevention of disease (Relman 1988). These are fundamental issues for the doctor–manager in a clinical specialty. Audit is a key process in providing some of the answers.

Audit can be considered under the following headings.

- medical or clinical audit;
- resources, resource management;
- research;
- teaching;
- quality.

The main purpose of this chapter is to describe *clinical audit*. This and the other forms are interrelated but the overall topic is best subdivided in this way for discussion.

Medical audit

Medical audit has been defined as the:
"Systematic, critical analysis of the quality of medical care, including the procedures used for diagnosis and treatment, the use of resources, and the resulting outcome and quality of life for the patient".

(Department of Health1989)

It was believed that an effective programme of audit would help to provide the necessary reassurance to doctors, patients and managers that the best possible quality of service is being achieved within the resources available. The White Paper (1989) recommended that audit should become part of routine professional practice (and in fact it has been since the 1991 Act) and, in particular, its use must form part of the training of junior staff. It was appreciated that the process of audit needed to be conducted within a clearly defined framework if it were to be fully effective.

For the doctor–manager, this should be a positive development, in that it provides a structural framework in which to review clinical practice and to assess the effectiveness of outcomes of medical care. Although primarily an educational, peer review activity, multidisciplinary audit can bring together all those professionals involved in the provision of medical care (senior and junior doctors, pharmacists, pathologists, etc.) to devise detailed protocols for the management of selected clinical conditions.

One benefit of bringing together key members of the team in a common purpose is that some of the traditional barriers created by total medical autonomy are opened up to debate and review. However, because of the potential loss of these traditional freedoms and possibly because of its association with business and accountancy, the word 'audit' is unpopular with many doctors. Some do not care for the implementation of guidelines or protocols because of their possible threat to clinical freedom. This is discussed on p. 99.

Medical and clinical audit

Medical audit and clinical audit are often used synonymously. Strictly speaking *medical* audit, as defined by the White Paper (1989), should involve itself with issues directly relating to or from medical intervention. '*Clinical* audit' might be considered to cover all aspects of clinical care, e.g. nursing, paramedical, etc., and is the form commonly adopted. All members of the team contribute to the audit process.

Clinical audit complements and may partly overlap with financial audit, utilisation review and management of resources, but is primarily clinical, not managerial; its focus is the process and results of medical care rather than the use of resources and it is the responsibility of doctors rather than managers. Most importantly, it is *local*.

The audit loop

Audit, as with profit and loss accounts in business, is an examination of activity that attempts to measure success or failure and to identify remediable shortcomings. The cybernetic loop (Fig. 4.1) is closed when action is taken to improve performance and future audit demonstrates that this has been achieved. At one end of the scale there are simple types of audit, such as aspects of waiting times, clinico-pathology conferences,

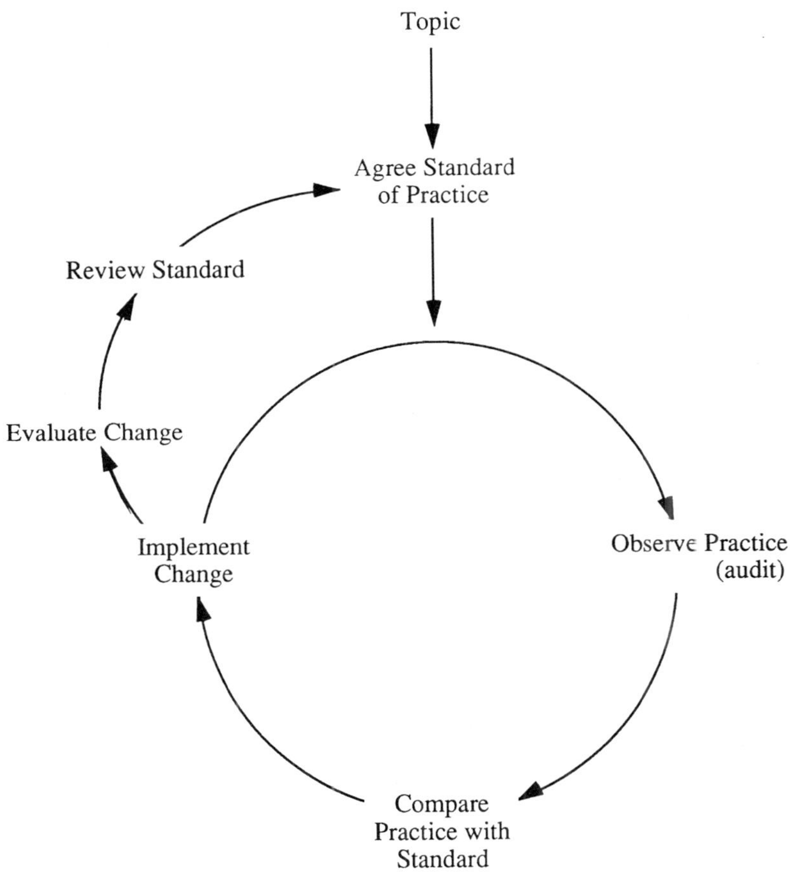

Figure 4.1 Audit loop

etc. At the other, a randomised controlled trial is a form of audit which may be seen as a gold standard.

One of the problems with clinical audit is that some outcomes cannot be measured easily, e.g. How do you measure some kinds of morbidity or the adverse effects of investigation?

Commitment to audit

Who should do it?

First, a fundamental principle has been that the quality of medical work can only be reviewed by a doctor's peers — although this is being questioned following a recent crisis where incorrect histopathology diagnoses appear to have been made over a number of years. The responsibility for and effectiveness of medical audit is discussed further in Chapter 7.

Medical audit does require specialised knowledge of current medical practice together with access to a system of adequate medical records. Professional leadership is therefore essential. So, the system should be medically led, with a local medical audit committee chaired by a senior clinician. The overall form of audit should be agreed locally between doctors and management; the latter needs to know that an effective system of medical audit is in place and that the work of each medical team is reviewed at regular and frequent intervals to be agreed locally.

Secondly, external audit is a much less powerful inducement to behavioural change than audit carried out by those who have a professional interest in the results. External audit that reports unfavourably is inevitably challenged or ignored. Audit is only effective in inducing change when carried out by those people who are required to undergo that change.

Time

Medical audit requires commitment in terms of the clinician's time, good and accessible medical records, adequate information and secretarial staff. The level of audit activity required of individual clinicians should be made explicit (in many areas this has been established, namely, one session per month). Two basic components are regular attendance at meetings of peers, at which records are kept, and planning and completion by each clinician of (say) one simple audit project per year. Those leading the audit process have the responsibility of keeping the programme interesting, entertaining and varied (so that staff are motivated).

Conflict with other responsibilities

There is already mounting pressure on a clinician's time in order to meet quality standards such as reducing waiting lists. Time for clinical and research work is curtailed. Probably the best method of avoiding too much loss of clinical work is to have a rolling programme of half-days for monthly audit across all disciplines, so that everything closes at once, e.g. theatre, anaesthesia, outpatients, etc. Nonetheless, valuable clinical time is lost and many clinicians who normally rely on peer group publications in reputable journals to direct them in their clinical management rather than looking at their own practice ask whether audit is necessary.

Of course, reading peer group publications does not mean that clinicians will necessarily follow ideal practice. A working definition of audit should be 'that process by which *actual* clinical practice is compared with ideal clinical practice' Audit is about ensuring that clinical work is up to, or close to, ideal clinical practice; so this means studying one's own practice.

Documentation

For audit to work properly it is essential that progress is documented and monitored. In some units it has been found that records are not kept (in about 50% in one report) and it is impossible to monitor whether any effective change has occurred.

Audit may involve the collection of a wide range of data from individual cases (e.g. maternal death enquiries); or may be a multicentre programme involving thousands of patients. This raises a number of problems: methods are not standardised; one group is doing it differently from the next. There should be an audit of audit; only this will eventually show which of the various models has proven to be the most useful.

Clinical freedom

If a doctor (professionally qualified and licenced by the GMC) genuinely believes that what he/she is doing for a patient is the best possible practice, then whatever that doctor does, it could be argued, is best practice. He/she is under no obligation to perform to any set, external standard, but applies clinical judgement in each case. This is sometimes termed clinical freedom. Audit encourages the establishment of guidelines and protocols which are a threat to clinical freedom. Fixed protocols may be seen to be even more threatening than guidelines — they provide precise instructions which should be followed. Guidelines and protocols may be introduced simply to force doctors, uncritically, to follow the same procedure for all patients with the same condition.

However, doctors must admit that there are major variations in clinical practice in treating patients with the same disorder in different areas. So, in practice peer review has been developed, i.e. whatever the majority thinks is correct is probably correct. Whilst this may be called 'sheep theory' it is fundamental to effective medical audit. A group of doctors meet to discuss management and judge by consensus whether management is appropriate.

If, via audit, a 'best' management policy were to emerge for a clinical condition, it would seem sensible to adopt a standard approach. This is all that a guideline would recommend. Is this loss of clinical freedom or acceptance of clinical responsibility?

Fundamentals of good audit

Good audit is intended to effect change. It is important that it is focussed and simple in design. The following questions should be asked at the start:

- *Why* is this particular audit being done? How and why was the topic selected? What are the objectives of the study?
- *How* is it to be done? What methods are to be used in achieving the objectives?

(and, at the end of the study)

- *What* did it find? How are the results to be interpreted in terms of improved health care?

(Crombie & Davies 1992)

Why?

In clinical audit the objective is to improve the quality of health care. Other purposes such as service planning and resource management complicate the process, dissipate effort and make it harder to do (Crombie & Davies 1992).

A major problem is the selection of topics. It is easy to fall into the trap of auditing too many activities at once, but there is a dilemma here. Unless an audit session is sufficiently full of varied clinical topics, it becomes useless as a training exercise for junior medical and non-medical staff. There probably should be a mixture of low-key review subjects, definitive audit and research progress review.

For definitive audit the topics chosen should be well-defined and amenable to standard-setting. For example, commonly performed surgical procedures in gynaecology — D&C and hysterectomy — are suitable subjects for study. Alternatively, high cost areas of activity (e.g. laser surgery) are equally suitable.

How?

The difficult stage in audit is setting standards: a statement has to be made about what is acceptable care and what is not. What is an acceptable wait for an outpatient appointment or for the length of stay in hospital? What is an acceptable rate of postoperative wound infection?

What targets should be set for acceptable care? The objective criteria for acceptable care (e.g. wound infection rate) are relatively easy to measure, but the subjective ones may not be recorded provided the final outcome is satisfactory (e.g. a patient may be recorded as having made a good recovery following treatment although many items in the recovery process (pain) might have been unrecorded or unreported). Very often clinical judgement decides whether the management of the case was satisfactory.

Motivation of staff, whereby they enthuse about the collection of data and attendance at meetings is important also. Those leading the audit process have the responsibility of keeping the programme interesting, entertaining and varied.

Should the study be on a fixed time scale (which fits in with an audit programme), or should it be on a fixed sample size (which is more like a research project and may allow a proper evaluation — statistical if necessary — at the end of the project)? The latter is more likely to be believed and therefore to succeed in effecting change.

Audit is very susceptible to bias, e.g. there may be non-response in a survey; patients' case notes may go missing; patients may fail to turn up for follow up. These factors need to be taken into account when final data are analysed.

What did the study find?

The analysis of data will be made easier if identifiable targets have been set at the start and if sample size and statistics have been considered in advance.

Unfortunately, the needs for change are not always recognised; and even if they are, there may be reluctance to remedy the deficiency. The in-built resistance to change, so prevalent in medicine, may cause referral to other units to see what is happening in them, before change is made in one's own directorate. Even then, lasting change is notoriously difficult to achieve (perhaps one should not seek lasting change but continuing change!).

Often too much is expected too soon. A number of audit reports only report the first cycle when little can have been accomplished. Progressive improvements in care over a period of time are more impressive. Good audit goes on to assess the impact of changes in practice.

Organisational framework for audit

The framework in which audit takes place is best described by reference to Figure 4.2. The District Medical Audit Committee's role is to plan and monitor: a comprehensive programme of medical audit; an annual forward programme for audit; an annual report on the previous year's audit activity. The Regional Committee's role is to advise on and support the development of audit across the Region. Local management (e.g. an NHS Trust) needs to see that an effective system of medical audit is in place in order to ensure that resourses are used in the most effective way (hence the overlap with resource management). Arrangements will need to be the same for self-governing hospitals as for DMUs, and for private sector units.

The doctor–manager and audit

If you take on a management role you have to be sensitive to the potential for using clinical audit to justify a 'management' policy, thereby discrediting the audit process. However, you have a great advantage over NHS managers in the potential to achieve changes in clinical practice to improve the standards of direct patient care. Doctors in management have the power and ability to divert resources within the department (provided they are there) to areas identified as being in need of additional investment.

The management responsibilities of facilitating audit within (say) a Directorate relate to:

- organising and collecting relevant data, which may be linked to computerised patient information systems, stand-alone departmental microcomputers or manual analysis of data;
- provision (and protection) of a budget to fund the audit process;
- ensuring that the lessons learned from audit are translated into departmental medical practice and form part of the educational process.

Whilst these may be your responsibilities, it is likely that they will be discharged through the departmental infrastructure, e.g. audit assistants can prove to be a valuable resource in advancing the broader implications of audit.

Resource management

There is inevitable overlap between *clinical audit* and *resource manage-*

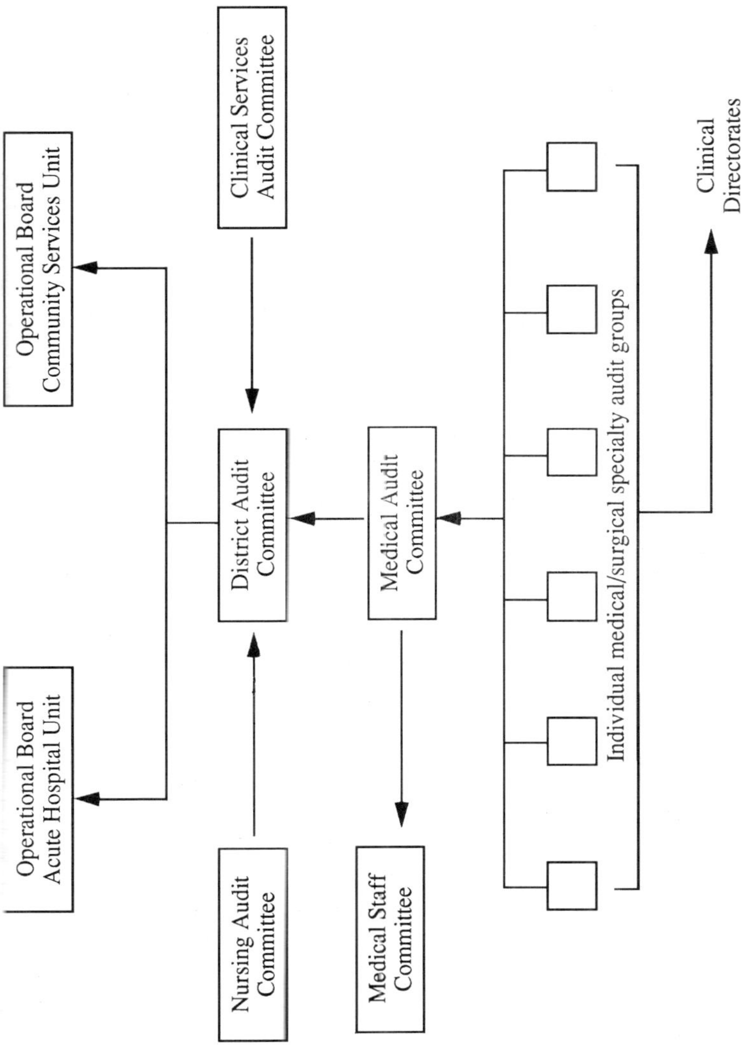

Figure 4.2 Organisational framework for audit

ment. The priorities of clinical audit are quality of clinical practice, training and education, and use of resources. Those for resource management are the same but in reverse order.

Similarities are:

- *Common basic clinical data* — both need complete, accurate recording, capture and encoding of diagnoses, complications, and procedures. So clinical supervision of data is needed; feedback to clinicians for verification; and consistent, comprehensive definitions and classifications.
- In medical organisation and behavioural terms, both need willingness and ability to *agree and respond to information*. Doctors find this hard.
- *Common costs for data capture and verification* e.g. clinical time, technical and clerical support and data handling (so these should be shared).

Differences are:

- *Reporting structure* — accountability for internal medical audit is primarily to your professional peer group; secondarily to management. The reverse is true for resource management.
- *Boundaries* — resource management focuses on a Directorate/Department; audit may cross managerial borders.
- *End users* — resource management is a tool for purchasers and providers to monitor contracts; audit focuses on clinical practice.

Resource management is primarily about the efficient use of resources but must include quality of care; more efficient use of resources will benefit quality. Clinical audit is primarily about improving the quality of care but will lead to more efficient use of resources, for instance, by reducing complications and decreasing length of stay (Editorial 1990).

Clinical audit may show inadequacies in service which are outside the control of the clinician, e.g. a surgeon may have an unusually high incidence of post-operative wound infections because of inexperienced junior staff, etc. Such a deficiency may be soluble by reallocation of resources within a Clinical Directorate or may need central funding. Another example is long waiting times, e.g. for hips. For this particular problem it can be proven, almost without audit, that better care could be provided with more resources.

The NHS has limited, finite, resources and the situation is likely to stay this way for some time. Under these circumstances the most equitable way of allocating limited resource is by identifying where there is objective clinical need. In the past clinicians could only 'shroud wave' to attract funds, the ones with the loudest voices coming off best. Clinical audit should even this out. If substandard practice is widespread because of underfunding, the clinician, using hard data from clinical audit, should have a strong tool for claiming extra resource.

There is a delicate balance in the inter-relationship of the features of clinical audit and resource management — management is concerned with efficiently achieving goals — and all those participating in audit are to some extent also involved in management. From a management perspective, clinical audit can stress and reinforce the common interest of a unit and can be used to determine collective policies for managing resources and providing services.

Research and education

Again there is overlap with clinical audit. The objective of audit is to survey local practice to see how it measures against agreed standards. The standards are set or developed through research. The same cybernetic loop pertains (see Fig. 4.1). Clinical audit and research projects both ask questions that relate to quality of care. Research determines what constitutes good care, whereas audit determines whether good care is being practised. Research seeks to define best practice by testing a hypothesis — which is then either proven or disproven. The result is an answer which can be applied throughout medical practice. Audit asks only, Is best practice being applied locally?

The methodology of audit is similar to that of research — unbiased data collection, objectivity. But the purpose of audit is limited — it is not concerned with establishing the most efficacious model of performance but only with surveillance of present practice and performance.

Would time be better spent on research work rather than clinical audit? The argument against this is that there is no point developing new standards (via research) if existing standards are not being met. In fact, audit ensures that standards set through research are being reached, and that the best clinical procedures, as defined by research, are being used. Research should be stimulated by audit as a retrospective review of clinical practice often generates hypotheses for improved treatment regimens. Research, audit and education overlap but should not be in competition (Fig. 4.3).

In summary, the differences between research, education and audit are:

- research defines best practice;
- education introduces best practice into everyday practice;

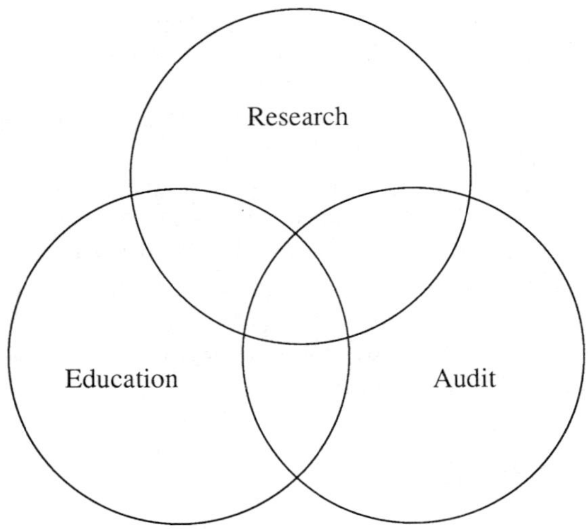

Figure 4.3 Overlap of audit with research and education

- audit determines whether best practice is occurring locally.

Or put another way:

- advances in clinical care need good research;
- implementing research findings needs education;
- effective education needs audit.

it can be seen all three are interrelated (Jacyna 1992, Jacyna et al 1992).

The *educational* implications of audit should be recognised because education is an important subsidiary aim, the process should be instructive.

Quality

The quality of care of patients can be audited in three dimensions:

- structure;
- process;
- outcome.

Structure

This can be defined as the availability of buildings, equipment and suitably qualified staff. Whilst structure may be readily audited, it is unlikely to be a good guide to quality of care, i.e. bad care can occur in well equipped hospitals.

Process

This refers to the activities of medical care, choice of operative procedure, length of stay and follow up. A review of hospital records audits the process of care and some immediate outcomes.

Outcome

This refers to the change in the patient's current and future state of health that can be attributed to the medical intervention episode of care. Unless the outcome is an improvement in the present or future health of a patient, the medical intervention has been meaningless, however fine the structure and however careful the process.

These three dimensions are complementary and do not rival measures of quality of care. However, as outcome measures (other than mortality) are difficult to define, much of the current activity in audit concentrates on the process of care as a proxy for outcome (Fig. 4.4).

Summary

Measurement is crucial for evaluating clinical practice and for planning. Often we do not do as we say we do and so an objective critical analysis is necessary.

We have described the fundamentals of good medical audit and the framework in which it is conducted. The overlap between audit and resource management, and between audit and research/education have been described in some detail. Quality has been mentioned here only briefly but is discussed further in Chapter 7.

Whilst the principles of audit are accepted, there remains some anxiety about whether it is being done properly; whether it has been thought out adequately in advance of legislation. This is discussed further in Chapter 7.

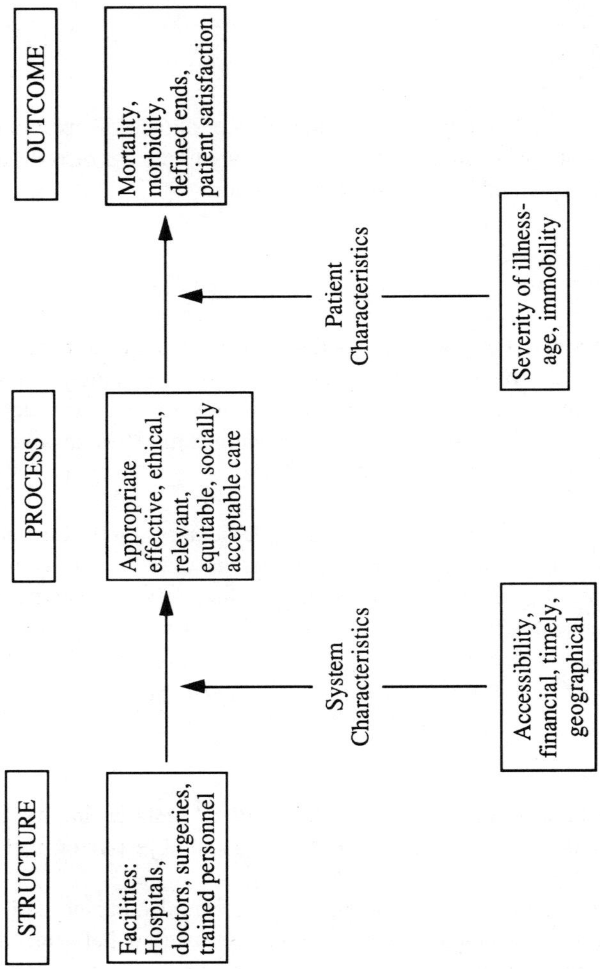

Figure 4.4 Schematic representation of dimensions to consider when measuring quality of care

Further reading

Crombie I K, Davies H T O
1992 Towards good audit. British Journal of Hospital Medicine 48: 182–185

Department of Health
1989 Working for Patients, Medical Audit (Working paper No.6). HMSO, London

Editorial 1990
Resource management and audit. British Medical Journal 301: 166

Jacyna M R
1992 Pros and cons of medical audit. . . . a conversation with a sceptic. Hospital Update July: 512–517

Jacyna M R, de Lacey G, Chapman E J
1992 How does medical audit differ from research? How necessary are computers? Hospital Update August: 592–596

Relman A
1988 Assessment and accountability: the third revolution in health care. New England Journal of Medicine 319: 1220–1222

Shaw C D, Costain D W
1989 Guidelines for medical audit: seven principles. British Medical Journal 299: 498–499

5 Managing people

Introduction

The purpose of this chapter is to provide guidelines for doctor–managers who wish to extend their clinical interpersonal skills to those needed for managing a workforce. The way in which you manage the people working for you is the most important factor contributing to the success of your organisation. As 75% of your revenue budget is accounted for by staff salaries, efficient management of staff is crucial. Some of the principles and applications of Human Resource Management (HRM) are considered below.

The range of occupations and professions within the NHS is huge compared with other organisations. There are doctors, nurses, engineers, technicians, computer staff, managers, finance officers, etc. The complexity is enhanced by political and economic factors, the influence of the professional organisations and unions. Managing such a wide range of occupations and professions is difficult.

Having an 'overview' of the needs of the team, you, as doctor–manager (in conjunction with your Business and Clinical Managers) are in a position to 'direct' the selection and interview process to some extent, thereby ensuring that the right person is chosen for the right job. Overseeing the construction of an induction programme for new staff should ensure that other staff are aware of the stresses of a new job; that new recruits gain in confidence from the start and thereby begin to contribute to the system from the start.

Principles of human resource management

Human Resource Management in the NHS is an integral part of every manager's job. The Personnel Specialist may have more of a role in strategic planning for the organisation as a whole but the day-to-day personnel issues are the responsibility of anyone who takes on a managerial role. For you the main concern is managing your own team. You will be responsible for some of this; you will need to delegate to other members of the Directorate management team as 'line managers' and sometimes even further — in fact, to the lowest level compatible with accountability. Line managers are in a prime position for assuming responsibility because they are likely to be the first to be aware of difficulties facing the team.

You need to have a working knowledge (via business and financial advisers) of staff salaries: costs of regular *vs* locum medical staff, overtime, Bank nursing staff; the cost implications of, say, a new Staff Grade appointment; the staffing costs needed for development programmes, etc. An integral part of managing people is appraising the team of the financial situation; of the constraints imposed by lack of funds, etc. Otherwise, they may expect far more of the system than is possible. However, they should also be made aware of the possibility of using Directorate funds in a way which can be exciting, e.g. development projects.

The 'bread and butter' aspects of HRM which have devolved, to a greater or lesser extent, to Clinical Directorates or their equivalents include recruitment and selection, induction, training and development, and promotion. These responsibilities are shared between members of the Directorate: for example, recruitment and selection are issues for the more senior Business and Clinical Managers to address, as are appraisal and promotion; induction, development and training belong to everybody on the team, with certain members being more influential than others in particular areas. In the induction of junior medical staff it is likely that a senior registrar or equivalent will take the lead, and so on.

The framework within which HRM is conducted at Directorate/ Specialty unit level is:

- recruitment;
- selection/interview/probation;
- induction;
- training and development;
- motivation, incentives;
- appraisal of progress;
- job design and analysis;
- team building;
- discipline, grievance procedures.

Although some of these are not your direct responsibility you will need to understand the procedures involved. Some are described briefly here and are applied to clinical groups later.

Recruitment

It goes without saying that successful recruitment depends on good applicants being available. In many areas there is a serious deficiency in 'raw material' (e.g. school leavers wanting to take up nursing) and this is likely to get worse over the next few decades.

In hospital practice it is tempting to blame ineffective training for poor recruitment to more senior posts, but it is not so much the training which is at fault as the poor rewards afterwards. For example, doctors are no longer prepared to endure long hours of duty and the stress of 24-hour on-call without adequate financial compensation, so they choose less onerous specialties, or even decide against medicine as a career (the real issue behind the current 'juniors' hours of duty' debate is better pay!).

As the fall in the number of young recruits to nursing and clerical jobs continues, managers will have to look at every means of increasing the supply of staff, of widening the labour field and of retaining their staff; for example, flexible hours of work, assistance with transport, relaxation of rigid pay structures must be considered.

Example.

With the change to our Trust's Terms and Conditions of Service from Whitley Council, there has been a shift towards replacing Nursing Auxiliaries with Health Care Assistants (HCAs). Auxiliaries have traditionally been higher paid than counterparts outside hospital (e.g. equivalent staff in nursing homes, etc.). The new grade gives comparable rates for the job (although less attractive conditions than per Whitley Council, obviously). There is no problem with recruitment of HCAs and so the labour pool can be increased and the Trust is able to employ 1.3 HCAs for each auxiliary.

Selection/interview

Considerable information about the candidate can, and should, be gained before the interview from every source available. Whilst good interview technique (by the interviewee) is important, selection on the basis of 'the best on the day' performance is out-dated. This can sometimes lead to the selection of a candidate who is good at being interviewed but nothing else. Similarly, because a candidate is good on paper, it does not necessarily follow that he/she will fit into the team.

The ability to sell the job is becoming more and more crucial in the light of the recruitment difficulties outlined above. The interviewing team should have a vision of what the job can offer the candidate as well as a clear picture of the qualities the candidate should have in order to meet the needs of the team. The interview should be conducted with these thoughts in mind in order to get the best out of the candidate at interview and to ensure that the right person is appointed. You should think 'team' and ask how the candidate will fit into it and if his/her broader view matches your own.

Within our Directorate there now seems to be more open discussion about who will fit in best with the rest of the team. The doctor–manager can coordinate the views of colleagues and present them to the Chief Executive, thereby bringing in support from Central Management.

Candidates may ask for advice on a number of issues at the end of the initial interview and you should be prepared for the questions. After junior doctors' interviews common questions relate to the hours of duty expected of them. In the current climate of changing duty hours and rotas they need to be clear that hours of duty, rotas, additional hours of duty (AHD) payments are continually having to be revised in order to fit in with revised national guidelines. The issue about junior doctors' hours of duty — which is a major problem at present because it has knock-on effects on the rest of the Directorate with regard to timetables, clinics to be covered, locums, etc. — is discussed on p. 129.

Probation

Taking on inexperienced junior staff who have no desire to fit into the team can be a serious and costly mistake. So a probationary period is becoming an accepted part of a job for all new personnel — except medical staff (although it is allowed for long-term locums). Because it applies to everyone else, the system may soon be widened to medical staff as well.

However, a probation period in senior posts is different and can be a very unsettling and unproductive time for someone who has had years of training. By this stage the selection process should have weeded out the less capable and there should probably be no need for it, but a limited tenure programme is still used in some academic posts, and is suggested for senior staff in the NHS, with equivalents of the Board exams in the USA being employed to ensure that a high standard of practice is maintained.

Induction

Induction is the introduction of a new employee to a new job. It is a great opportunity to convey to the new employee what the Department is all about. The sooner new staff feel they are contributing to the organisation the better. Contribution is the key to motivation and vice versa. A staff member needs to know why he/she is doing the job and how the job fits into the overall organisational plan/philosophy.

A new job may be a frightening experience in which the recruit may be particularly anxious about failure. If left to flounder on his/her own, there will be a longer time before he/she contributes to the system. A good induction programme will smooth the *transition* phase from the confidence of having succeeded at interview to the entirely new and perhaps lowly status in the new job. First impressions are lasting; a bad induction programme may produce negative feelings at the start which then persist.

Example.

The main concern of some junior doctors in Obstetrics is the need to complete the requirements of Vocational Training Scheme training in order to get on the Obstetric list. There is a fault in the system whereby job satisfaction assumes a secondary priority and this arises largely because there is little time available for tuition. So a lack of motivation develops.

The induction programme has to be swift, well-organised and acceptable to the trainees. For example, the induction process for junior medical staff has to be hurried and revised and updated every 6 months because their contracts are only short-term. We stagger the information given to new staff over the first few weeks of their new jobs, the object being not to overload them on the first day. Feedback from previous trainees has also helped identify the items of instruction needed early in the job, e.g. an immediate introduction to labour ward nursing staff is important for new obstetric trainees.

The first induction sessions should give the new employee, e.g. a junior doctor, the following information:

- introduction to staff (e.g. to nursing staff);
- general nature of job to be done;
- supervisor (SR);
- job description;
- description of the organisation;
- department rules, protocols, safety measures;
- coding (which is assuming paramount importance following the NHS reforms), communication with GPs.

There must then be a second session for *feedback*.

Training

Training should be regarded as an *investment* rather than a *cost*, because of its positive effect on performance. It has to be *continuous* on account of rapid change — both in organisational management and in technology.

> **Example.**
>
> The need for continuous training programmes has become particularly clear in our Directorate since the advent of resource management, the implementation of IT and computer systems, and new developments in medical care. For example:
>
> - secretaries have had to learn to use word processors (very often temporary staff have had insufficient training in the system);
> - managers must make full use of IT;
> - doctors have to use various computer systems for the purposes of medical audit;
> - some jobs have changed and expanded — particularly where there has been devolution of responsibility from one area to another. This has applied particularly to administrative and clerical staff with the implementation of practice management and the devolution of medical records;
> - there have been changes in priority in the organisation, e.g. the development of minimally invasive surgery, a shift towards outpatient procedures, the development of a pregnancy counselling service.

Training methods and availability

Training must be tailored to suit individual needs. For many members of the Directorate (i.e. most of the non-clinical staff), in-house or on-the-job training may be the most satisfactory. This has the advantage of matching training against departmental needs, but it may have the disadvantages of familiarity and preconceived opinions.

'In-house' training is probably best accomplished by the line manager or his/her equivalent or deputy. However, other teachers should be sought from amongst existing personnel. Hospitals have a wealth of different skills on site which can provide a rich internal resource for training. Exploited fully this resource enables training to be varied and innovative.

External or off-the-job training (e.g. courses, external lectures) tends to give a broader perspective. Cross-fertilisation of ideas is possible. However, external training may prove to be very expensive relative to the value of what is learned. Other disadvantages are that teaching is pitched at the lowest common denominator and is not matched to staff or the organisation. A way round this problem is to ask a person who has already been on a particular external course to assess its value. Then you can tailor-make a course for your own department using internal resources.

It is unlikely that training in all of the specialty and subspecialty areas can be provided on site, so trainees should be made aware (by the line manager) of external training and be encouraged to join if appropriate. It may be necessary to buy-in external training or provide a mix of the various forms.

Example.

A particular training need which has arisen during the last few years and requires both external and internal modes is surgical training for senior staff. The trend towards minimally invasive surgery has meant that senior, experienced surgeons have had to learn a completely new approach to their work. The techniques involved in laser and laparoscopic surgery are immensely different from anything they have done before. A combination of external (course) training with the passing-on of information learned to fellow colleagues seems to be the best way of providing this particular need. In our Directorate we have chosen to invite experienced operators to give in-house training also.

Evaluation of training programmes

Even though an investment, training is expensive. One has to consider the trainer's and trainee's time and the training available. At present external medical training is not evaluated carefully. At most a verbal or written report on the course is requested. 'In-house' training also needs to be validated and checked against objectives. For both, new skills need to be reinforced back in the workplace. The cost-effectiveness of the programme should be checked to decide whether the resource allocation was justified.

Example.

In our Directorate we are working towards the development of a Departmental Training Strategy. Resource requirements specifically needed for training must be identified and presented to the Central Executive as part of our Annual Business Plan. Until now service requirements have assumed priority but must change if quality of service is to be maintained. Consultant and senior nurse retraining is an important feature of such a strategy.

The evaluation of a training programme should allow modification of the training plans of future trainees in a way designed to make them meet aims and objectives more effectively, i.e. training should be continually revised.

The responsibility for training programmes within a Directorate or specialty arena is not entirely yours; but you are in a position to oversee the whole development of the department and are probably best equipped to spot deficiencies in the training programmes — particularly those provided for medical staff.

The provision of funding for the retraining of senior staff has not yet received sufficient attention. The emphasis hitherto has been to devote training resource to staff members in the 'training grades'. However, senior staff (medical and nursing) need extra training in order to keep up to date with new developments. For example, senior surgeons are having to learn new endoscopic techniques; senior nurses have to adapt to the changes imposed by IT (and their jobs may be on the line if they fail).

Funding for these aspects of retraining is not available unless it is found within the Directorate by virement of resources.

Performance appraisal

In the non-clinical arena there is an annual *appraisal interview* and this is being introduced into the clinical scene also. For non-clinical staff, appraisal is the responsibility of the line manager or Directorate Business Manager; for nursing staff, the Clinical Nurse Manager; and for junior medical staff, the consultant of the 'firm' (how this will work in the future if firms are dissolved secondary to shift system duties is not yet clear). Appraisal should be more than a brief chat: there should be adequate preparation beforehand.

In the medical arena (e.g. junior medical staff), whilst objective appraisal can be gained from the keeping of log-books; examination successes; the completion of certified courses; the assessment of surgical expertise and experience, it often helps to glean information from other sources (e.g. senior nursing staff). For non-medical posts the reliance is more on performance against agreed objectives.

A useful technique in junior medical staff appraisal (and this is probably applicable to other groups) is to get them to rank their own performance first, using the guidelines which you will use later. This self-appraisal exercise can be interesting, because many medical staff overrate themselves by recording 'excellent' against many of the aspects of performance being measured! This means that for them there is no room for improvement. Travelling through a 'self-marked' appraisal exercise with a junior doctor is a less embarrassing way of broaching a discussion about his/her deficiencies in training than having a head-on confrontation. This approach should make it easier to give constructive criticism if it is necessary.

In summary, the person being appraised should be clear about:

- what good performance is;
- what his/her performance was against this definition;
- the nature of his/her strengths and weaknesses;
- how he/she might improve performance further;
- what development is desirable/required.

Independent performance review

The NHS reforms enabled Independent Performance Review (IPR) to be introduced into the NHS. Senior managers have a static spinal point on a salary scale (not incremental) and are judged (and paid) year on year according to the achievement of preset objectives. Hence you will find yourself in the position of having to grade other professionals on their performance (e.g. senior nurses, Business Manager). The process is overviewed by the Chief Executive, but it is not an easy task to measure the performance of senior nurses and managers.

Having said that, there should be nothing different here from some of your other duties such as examining for higher professional examinations. In these situations there are a set of guidelines (e.g. marks allocated for performance) which have to be followed. Providing that similar rules are followed for IPR (i.e. marks against the achievement or otherwise of preset objectives), there should be no difficulty.

This whole issue generates a lot of unease amongst doctors, particularly when they foresee it being applied to themselves. It is difficult, at this stage, to see how IPR could be applied to senior doctors. For example, how would you agree to measurement by set objectives? So much of senior doctors' work can only be assessed subjectively.

Job satisfaction

The most important ingredient in developing and motivating staff to expand the job and achieve more is *job satisfaction*. Other motivators such as incentives and promotion are powerful but not as important as this. Employees should be encouraged to do more than the job currently demands and this will not be done (properly) unless they want and enjoy the challenge. Extra potential should be spotted and realised — even if it means promoting the person to another job outside the immediate organisation. Most of all, the job should be made so satisfying that the individual employee is keen to assume this extra responsibility. The job may need to be continually redesigned to give better job satisfaction.

Many successful businesses are those where employees are shareholders and have a vested interest in making the organisation work. The sense of *ownership* is vitally important but is hard to achieve in the NHS which has such a large workforce. How do you generate job satisfaction when there is no promotion or perks? One way is by making staff feel that they have done a job well, and this is easier to achieve in a Directorate system where the numbers are small enough for you to walkabout and praise/congratulate staff on their work.

Non-financial (perks) and financial incentives (e.g. percentage bonuses linked to performance) do have a place, provided that such incentives *are* linked to performance and provided that there is a good chance of their being realized.

As mentioned earlier, a major incentive for junior doctors is pay, whilst for senior doctors it is often the sense of achievement from having done a job well (by and large, this is why Clinical Directors do the job). The achievement philosophy should be activated within the Directorate. Employees should know that their performance is good and worthwhile and worthy of promotion even if promotion is not possible. Feedback of good performance to them is important. This is the philosophy of Total Quality Management (TQM, see p. 166).

Promotion

Upwards

This usually depends on vacancies occurring elsewhere in the NHS — and, for medical staff, the number of these depends upon RHA and Government rules regarding staffing levels. For clinical medical staff there are rules relating to 'Achieving a Balance' and consequent restrictions imposed by the Regional Manpower Committee. For managers in the NHS, promotion to a more demanding job is to some extent outside Directorate control, and good Units/Trusts will have management development programmes to enable employees with potential to gain experience and skills which will enhance their performance. RHAs may also have graduate training schemes to 'nurture' managers of the future (from all professional backgrounds). For both doctors and managers, a degree of professional mobility is to be expected and desired.

Rotation (e.g. registrar rotation)

This is really an *experience increment* rather than promotion, but does prevent stagnation. It is important that doctors and managers exploit all rotation opportunities to encourage development.

> **Example.**
>
> We have started to rotate hospital and community midwives' duties: the result should be to keep them all up-to-date.
>
> Also, because of subspecialty development in Surgery, a number of ward-based nurses have developed into specialist nurses, and a plan has been devised to train a core group of nurses to work throughout the specialty, i.e. inpatient or ward-based, theatre and outpatient.

Above all, promotion must be seen to be fair. It can be a powerful incentive, although it may generate envy amongst those who are not eligible, e.g. many secretaries and administrative and clerical staff. Furthermore, many clinical staff are less interested in promotion now than previously. For them other personal factors are as important as promotion — which brings us back to job satisfaction being the most important motivator.

Job design and redesign

Principles of good job design

A *well-designed* job should:

- be reasonably varied and demanding;
- offer progressive learning;
- require some decisions and discretion;
- enable support of and by colleagues (rotas);
- recognise efforts;
- show how work fits in with corporate objectives;
- show it to be worthwhile;
- lead to some desirable future.

Job redesign

The implementation of the Trust status in hospitals has made it easier to change jobs to suit the needs of the organisation and this is beginning to happen across the board, i.e. with administrative and clerical staff, in the nursing field and, to some extent, in medicine (particularly with consultant staff).

Job redesign for most staff is usually done by someone other than the doctor–manager (e.g. Business Manager, Nurse Manager), although you must understand why it is necessary and how it fits in with departmental strategy.

Some of the questions you must ask when considering the redesign of jobs to suit manpower needs are:

- can a job be shared, can work be better organised?
- can there be redeployment between jobs/activities?
- is there evident underemployment or significant overtime?
- will anticipated changes in service require new skills and methods?
- do all staff have to be full time?
- are some staff overstretched; others not?

There are many areas where jobs and responsibility for a particular task can be shared. There is often overlap between nursing staff, paramedical staff, clerical staff and other ancillary workers. It is possible that the roles of physiotherapists and occupational therapists will be amalgamated; also those of practice nurse, district nurse and health visitor (*core curriculum concept*). With teamwork there should be less need for clearly demarcated jobs so such amalgamations might be very useful, particularly in the community. However, job content is a very sensitive issue and any change has to be handled carefully.

'Purification' of the job. In the junior doctor and nurse arena there has been considerable attention given recently to *purifying* jobs, i.e. eliminating the non-clinical duties which have for so long been expected of junior medical staff, nurses and medical students, e.g. portering, clerical duties, phlebotomy. The Heads of Agreement on Junior Doctors' Hours called for guidance on which suitable administrative, clerical or technical staff might undertake certain tasks now inappropriately performed by doctors in training, e.g.:

- locating empty beds for admissions (emergency and otherwise);
- routinely completing and delivering requests for and obtaining results of laboratory and other investigations;
- undertaking portering duties;

- providing a routine phlebotomy service;
- undertaking duties more appropriate to ward clerks such as filing results in case notes.

On the one hand staff should be encouraged to *extend* their jobs; on the other they should not be doing jobs which are more appropriately done by other people. But the purification approach may undermine the teamwork needed for current medical care.

New skills. Some areas of change which demand new skills from staff have been referred to already, e.g. information technology and the development of minimally invasive surgery. Arising out of these changes may be a need for new types of clerical and nursing staff. Nursing jobs, more than any, will have to move towards either subspecialty/high-dependency nursing or auxiliary status as the shift towards day- and outpatient surgery progresses and as the shift towards primary care services (via GP fundholding) impacts on hospital staffing levels. Similar changes will apply to the non-surgical specialties.

There are some very highly trained and well-motivated staff in nursing. Often they are used simply as chaperones. In the Outpatient Clinic their role can be extended to the performing of certain minor procedures; for example, in Gynaecology this can include the taking of cervical smears or becoming involved with subspecialty work.

Example.

In our Directorate there are subspecialty interests (amongst others) in infertility and Urogynaecology. Because of the nature of the investigations required and their timing, most infertility patients became 'ward attenders'. This was very unsatisfactory because it disrupted ward routine. Furthermore, the work involved in counselling these patients was not recorded (ward attenders have never been satisfactorily charted in the NHS — even though several thousand of them may be seen per year). We appointed a nurse as 'Infertility Coordinator'. This has had a tremendous impact on the organisation of the infertility programme.

In Urogynaecology the training of a nurse to manage the Urodynamics Unit has meant that we can see far more patients than ever before. The situation now is that she, together with a physiological measurement technician, can do many of the tests by themselves, thereby relieving pressure on medical staff.

Part-time jobs. Not all jobs need to be full-time and there is evidence that more and more people are keen to do sessional rather than full time work (e.g. doctors and nurses with young children, technical and paramedical staff, some GPs who want to devote part of their time to primary care and part to hospital work).

Team building and team work

Team building is the framework within which *team work* is accomplished. Team work is the actual activity. As part of the induction process a new employee should feel that he/she is a useful part of the existing team as soon as possible. Some background information should be circulated about the new member of the team and what the plans are for him/her to fit in with the rest.

Giving a group the responsibilty for completing a task is a useful way of pooling individual skills. Different tasks can be allocated within the team depending on capabilities. Such exercises may need a facilitator (manager) and resources to link with the wider organisation but the essence of group working is cooperation and team spirit.

The establishment of working parties to study particular problems in depth is a useful way of delegating responsibility to teams. It also saves time during Directorate meetings where lengthy discussion on one topic may not be appropriate.

Example.

A working party was established to conduct a feasibility study for a 5-day ward in surgery. The team comprised the Business Manager, Senior Registrar, Senior Nurse, Clerical Officer, i.e. representatives from all disciplines were asked to address the issue. With this team (which transcended hierarchy and disciplines and gave a complete picture of all potential problems and benefits), it seemed possible to change one ward to a 5-day unit. The team produced a joint report which was presented to the Directorate. The ground work was done and the Directorate approved the recommended actions. From there it was easy to implement the move swiftly and successfully.

Communication

For team work to operate successfully the following should apply:

- Everyone in the organisation should know his/her job and his/her immediate line manager — who should conduct the performance review and provide motivation, advice, help.
- There should be an adequate cascade of information (up and down) through *team briefing*, non-business events and social occasions.
- There should be dedicated time for developing operational policies, which later should release time and resources for treating patients.

- Whenever possible, managers and doctor–managers should visit people in their own departments ('walking the job'). However, walkabouts are time-consuming and care must be taken not to lose equally important patient time. Nevertheless, it is rewarding to make time for staff issues inside their own territory, where they feel less threatened if they raise controversial management issues for discussion.

Discipline and grievances

Disciplinary activities are part of the day-to-day function of a line manager (usually Business and Nurse Managers); doctor–managers have thus far been rarely involved. However, they should be aware of the management processes involved. Furthermore, disciplinary action needs also to be viewed in a broader context, i.e. the Trust.

The stages of a disciplinary procedure are as follows:

counselling
↓
investigation → no further action
↓
informal action
↓
review
↓
action needed
↓
formal stage (Personnel Department)

An alternative presentation would be:

Informal counselling
↓
investigation
↓
action
↓
review → no further action
↓

Formal investigation
↓
formal warning(s)
↓
review → no further action
↓
sanctions

Disciplinary action is needed if conduct is potentially dangerous or costly; if conduct encourages others to copy; if job performance is compromised; if other workers are affected; if authority is undermined; or if disciplinary rules are breached. An informal stage demands good counselling skills plus a reprimand in private. As with potential medicolegal issues, if the problem is nipped in the bud by timely counselling, there is no escalation of the crisis and no grievance procedure follows. Records are very important to show how the situation was handled (note the similarities with medicolegal cases).

Grievance procedures and employee rights

Again it is unusual for you, as doctor–manager, to be directly involved in these issues. You will have access to professional personnel advice and without it you should not tackle them. It could compromise future disciplinary proceedings if the 'technical' details are not strictly followed. For example, if a case goes to tribunal all interviews are examined and often cases dismissed on technicalities.

Manpower planning

In simple form this means:

- analysing current resources;
- forecasting future needs;
- making plans to supply the needs.

or ensuring the right number of the right people are in the right place at the right time.

The NHS differs from other employers: it is a labour-intensive service based on personal contact between staff and patients; technological advances in the NHS tend to *increase* the need for specialist staff, compared with industry where the opposite happens; as professional staff increase their degree of specialisation, there is a greater need for coordinators of service. Also, as professionals become more insistent on undertaking only professional duties and tasks, there is an increased demand for support from clerical, secretarial and technical staff.

At organisational level, it is important to have information on current 'manpower stocks'. One may need to have a detailed head count — laying down clearly the number of posts within the department by job title and salary. Information such as this may be difficult to interpret. For example, we commissioned a study to measure staffing levels in our Directorate and identified 14 different sources for manpower information . . . and all of them gave different information!

The number of people working in your unit needs to be continually reviewed. It cannot be assumed that whatever numbers and grades of staff are currently in post are there forever and, indeed, some may not need to be there forever and it may be wrong to recruit to an old vacancy. With the fundamental shift of some aspects of patient care from hospital to General Practice there is no doubt that manpower (particularly nursing) levels in hospital will have to decrease dramatically.

The following information is needed and should be supplied by a support manager/personnel department in order that decisions can be made by clinicians relative to perceived service needs:

- How many employees are there?
- What grades are they?
- What age are they?
- What are they paid?
- What vacancies are outstanding?
- What else could they do?

With regard to forecasting future manpower needs and making plans to supply those needs, it is the responsibility of the Directorate to ensure that the right number of staff are in-house. Only in this way can quality of patient care be assured. It may be difficult if resources are limited, but it is your job as doctor–manager to ensure that you have sufficient staff to maintain quality of patient care.

The questions often asked by Central Executive are 'Are you sure you are not overmanned?'; 'Are you sure you cannot close part of your unit at weekends?' These questions are difficult to answer: it may be that some 'job purification' will ease the situation: but gut feeling is that there are never enough staff; we always seem to be precariously balanced on a knife edge where any unexpected staff absence (e.g. sick leave) causes severe disruption of the service. With regard to weekend work a totally opposite view might be more appropiate: rather than closing wards at weekends to save staff costs, it might be more sensible to *use* weekend time more effectively by opening wards and theatres. At a time when waiting lists are long, when patients want their operations done at a time to suit them, weekend work should perhaps be encouraged and bed closures discouraged.

Example.

There is always significant overtime in our Directorate; in common with other surgical specialties there are so many variables in the provision of patient care, e.g. in the operating theatre there are patient and anaesthetic cancellations, portering shortages, broken equipment, unexpected crises during the course of surgery. A statistical 'episode' with the same operation code may take anything from 15 minutes to 3 hours to complete. There is also the need for continuity of care. Doctors cannot 'down-tools' in the middle of an operation so financial provision has to be made for this.

A contrasting example is provided by the saving of nursing time by shortening the shift overlap. At the time this was introduced into our hospital there was intense opposition, but it has been shown to work, without any detriment to patient care.

Establishing future manpower needs is difficult for a number of reasons other than the ones given as examples above. The traditional formulae for deciding the number of staff for the job (from work study) are too mechanistic. All individuals are different (e.g. some nurses have subspecialty knowledge). Redundancy may select all nurses over 55 but they are the ones with most experience and so possibly more help is needed to cover their absence. The data about present manpower stocks may be deficient, unobtainable or unreliable (as described in the example above). As well as changes in departmental objectives there will be a corporate plan for the whole Hospital/Trust which may override your ideas about what is needed (we lost a manpower information expert in a Trust redundancy programme; we lost an extremely useful Directorate financial adviser via promotion to a different Directorate).

There are external factors outside your control such as junior doctors' hours of duty, changing technology and changing rates of pay. There is the impact of the Patients' Charter, GP purchasers and the requests for peripheral clinics. Some of these are changing the face of the organisation faster than this book can be written!

The examples of job redesign quoted earlier indicate how jobs have to change in the new circumstances. These approaches to manpower planning are essential if future staffing levels are to be met.

Application of HRM to other professionals

Doctors

The number of doctors in the Health Service is approximately 61 000 (1989). Although they comprise only 5% of directly employed staff, they have great influence over the way resources are used.

Hours of duty

The two issues that relate to junior staff management are *hours of duty* and *training/career structure*. From the start of the NHS there has been the problem of providing an acceptable hospital career and training structure, while at the same time employing enough non-consultant staff to provide adequate out of hours emergency cover. 'Achieving a Balance — Plan for Action' (1987) was an agreement intended to improve the hospital career structure. The numbers of doctors in the training grades (Senior Registrar and Career Registrar) would be carefully controlled by the Joint Planning Advisory Committee (JPAC). However, it was estimated from RHA returns and from JPAC figures that to improve all unsatisfactory rotas such that hours could be reduced to acceptable levels could require as many as 2500 additional doctors in the training grades! There would be no prospect of an acceptable career structure with this number.

The Ministerial Group on Junior Doctors' Hours (DoH 1990) recommended that the long hours — both in total and in continuous stretches of duty — still worked by many hospital doctors in training must be reduced. The subsequent working arrangements for doctors in training agreed by the Joint Negotiating Committee for Hospital Medical and Dental Staff was circulated as a set of documents by the NHS Management Executive in mid-1991. (The reader is referred to these documents for details of the proposed maximum periods of duty and minimum periods of off-duty.) In brief there is a requirement to reduce the average contract hours for on-call doctors in hard-pressed posts to 72 per week by December 1994 and on-call doctors in all posts to the same amount by December 1996.

The mechanisms for change whereby these reductions in hours might be achieved without increasing the numbers of doctors in training include the introduction of shift or partial shift systems, arranging time off after a night on duty, reducing the number of tiers of junior cover or increasing cross-cover between specialties and employing more part-time doctors, staff-grade doctors and consultants.

Clinical services

Any mechanism of shifts or partial shifts will reduce the number of doctors on duty during the normal working day. It is envisaged that this extra daytime work will be picked up by career-grade staff such as consultants and staff-grades (and possibly hospital practitioners). Thus the manpower demand is for career grade rather than training-grade doctors. This is a *fundamental* difference from the demand for additional training grade doctors that arises from improved rotas.

Also, the strong encouragement towards some sort of shift system will end the 'firm' system so long established in hospital practice, and consultants will need to share the resource of junior staff, adopting more of a 'team' approach. The *individual* status of a consultant — say his/her ability through special expertise to attract high class junior doctors to his/her team — may be lost. The junior doctor group will be a pool, rather like a typist pool. It can be argued that this is detrimental to patient care and postgraduate training.

Training

The change of hours of duty of junior doctors which takes them further away from daytime work where supervised training is available, means that there has to be some provision to compensate for this — be it extra hours of payment for training during overlap periods, designated periods in each week for intense postgraduate training or external courses. There will need to be additional resources for teaching.

Whilst total or partial shift systems may not be suitable for junior staff training they are likely to be particularly inappropriate for those in higher medical specialist training because daytime duties are removed. This is the time when they learn most from their seniors. It may be possible to build dedicated and protected teaching time into the new system, but the whole issue of continuing postgraduate education in the new system is causing concern at Royal College level and amongst senior consultants. The RCOG is not yet convinced that 72 hours is adequate for education beyond General Professional Training. It is this College's view that the main way of resolving the excessive hours issue is an increase in staff at the SHO and intermediate levels. In practice this is happening: the moratorium on SHO numbers is being deregulated in a number of

Regions; and there is an expansion of intermediate grade doctors in the Staff Grade and in Visiting Registrar posts.

> **Example.**
>
> Ours is a busy obstetric unit delivering approximately 5000 babies/year. There are also a large number of gynaecology emergency admissions. There were 9 SHOs working a 1 in 3 without prospective cover. By taking on an extra (locum or temporary) SHO, whose duties were the same as the rest and whose College recognition was assured, we were able to change the rota to 1 in 4.5 and reintroduce prospective cover. Effectively this brings the rota to about 1 in 3 which is the present requirement of our Royal College for training purposes. The junior staff are happy with this. The move has ensured adequate cover and (in the main) has obviated the anxiety of finding and paying for locums.

> **Example.**
>
> The problem with registrars has been more difficult to solve. However, we have Regional Task Force approval for another consultant (bid for against the need to reduce doctors' hours). We have been able to fund — on the back of waiting list initiative money — a Staff Grade doctor (subsequently promoted to Associate Specialist) and (partly funded by a new pregnancy counselling service) a research fellow (visiting Registrar status). Reducing junior doctors' hours contributed to the salary of a Research Registrar. By incorporating the two 'visiting' registrars into the on-call rota, and by realignment of consultant clinics and registrar backup, we will be able to reduce each of the registrar's weekly hours to 72 per week.

There is a call from many quarters for more consultant supervision of junior staff, e.g. in the labour ward, partly for training and partly because of escalating litigation; consultants are being asked to devote more sessional time during the working day to the training and career counselling of junior doctors; as part of the Patients' Charter it is expected that there be less delegation of Outpatient consultations to junior staff; GPs (particularly fundholding GPs) demand more involvement by consultants, and so on. But if the answer to the problems of supervision is to appoint more consultants and the level of experience gained by them whilst in the training grades is low, their supervision will be of questionable value.

Nurses and midwives

In 1989 there were over 500 000. This is the largest staff group in the NHS comprising nearly half the workforce. It includes trained staff

(RGN,EN) and also Health Care Assistants and Nursing Auxiliaries whose training varies from place to place.

In the past there has always been a strong hierarchical system in the nursing profession, i.e. Matron/District Nurse Officer downwards. Issues which were previously addressed by the nursing hierarchy now have to be understood by the doctor–manager . The Clinical Nurse Manager will deal with day-to-day administration of the ward and its nursing staff, but the ultimate budgetary responsibility for staff levels in nursing and midwifery lies with you. This is a fundamental change. It has been a culture shock for senior nurses: they now have to report to you rather than the Head Nurse.

The extent of influence held previously by nurses is reflected in the size of nursing budgets: nurses and midwives take up the largest proportion of the salaries and wages bill; the cost of the nursing workforce amounts to over a quarter of the total current revenue expenditure of the NHS.

Patient care is largely done by nurses. They have a constant and direct contact with patients (albeit in shifts). Nurses give more personal care than most other groups of staff. In spite of working shifts, they seem to have overcome the lack of continuity of care (which is heralded as a major retrograde step by doctors facing the same need for reducing hours of duty) probably because there is an efficient, well-organised hand-over period.

Because of the responsibility and the need to provide 24-hour continuity of care, nurses are often under a great deal of stress. Not only are there the medical crises which are familiar to all clinical personnel (e.g. patients dying), but also pressures due to a more rapid turnover of patients with shorter length of stay. Reducing the length of stay may be beneficial to the patient, and financially sound to the manager (it may be possible to close a ward part of the time), but it means that patients are increasingly high-dependency cases. There is also an increase in the level of technical skill required by the nurse who is encouraged to extend his/her role and take over some of the duties which used to be done by doctors. Overall, there has been a relative increase in the workload for every nurse.

Also, there is the increasing shortage of qualified nurses and difficulties with recruitment. The projected fall in the number of young people coming into nursing in the 1990s has happened. The number of school leavers is falling and it is unlikely that enough of them can be recruited into nursing to maintain present nursing staff levels (to do so, it has been estimated that a third of all school leavers will need to be recruited!). Furthermore, Project 2000 will exacerbate the problem because student nurses will spend less time on the wards.

As well as these difficulties with recruitment, there have been arguments over pay and regrading. Although the latter was intended as a reward system and to offer a better career structure it appears, in many people's eyes, to have misfired. Appeals against the new grading are still going on and it has been estimated that they will take 14 years to clear!

So, the change to being 'managed' by a doctor–manager on top of all this is something which many nurses (particularly senior nurses) find difficulty in accommodating. Even inside directorate systems (and particularly where there are large numbers of nursing staff, e.g. midwifery), there will be concealed information relating to nursing staff numbers, salaries and grading points. It will take some time for the new structure to be appreciated. In practice, a totally *open* approach to staff problems discussed within the Directorate Management Team on a weekly basis is more likely to provide a solution than having to shunt the problem through many hierarchical committees.

Administrative and clerical staff

This group makes up the third largest group of staff employed in the NHS after nurses and ancillary staff. These staff cover a wide range of activity. Included in the group are laundry managers, managers of supplies, finance, personnel departments; clerical and secretarial staff working within clinical areas to support professional and technical staff.

Medical records staff and medical secretaries support clinical staff by relieving them of administrative, clerical and secretarial tasks and so allow them to concentrate on matters for which they have been professionally trained. The number of these staff should (but do not usually do so) go up as clinical staff numbers increase. Theirs is the essential work of coordinating and organising services, collecting and processing information. The NHS generates a vast amount of information. In recent years developments in information technology have caused many Health Authorities and Trusts to introduce computerised patient administration systems, so a number of medical records tasks have become automated. The benefits of such systems have, in many instances, as yet to be realised.

Professional and technical staff

Scientific and technical staff in professions allied to medicine (e.g. physics, computer science) is a growth industry because of the increasing needs for specialist skills resulting from developments in medical science and technology. Compared with industry, technological advances in the NHS tend to increase the need for specialist staff rather than the reverse. Furthermore, as the degree of specialisation increases there is a greater need for coordinators of the service.

This is a very varied group of people. Their work complements that of doctors and nurses and they are often supervised by doctors. People like chiropodists and ECG technicians have become an integral part of hospital life. Others, such as computer scientists, have hitherto had a less recognised role but are becoming increasingly important. Directorates will have to find resources to employ more of such people to facilitate, for example, medical audit.

Example.

One Directorate team became increasingly aware of the need for a Financial Assistant (PFA) attached whole-time to the Directorate. Originally, this was regarded by Central Management as too innovative to be considered seriously (even though the Directorate budget exceeded £5m). Since then, and having proved the post would be self–financing, it has been possible to appoint a PFA.

Other staff, supplies, stores, estates, etc.

The Directorate team will need, during the course of most working days, to liaise with staff from Supplies and Stores (most of these transactions are done through the Business Manager). For example, Medical and Surgical Supplies is an item on each month's spreadsheet and on the agenda of each week's Directorate team meeting and it usually generates some debate.

Similarly, there has to be rapport with the Estates Department. Now that subspecialty interests are developing in the surgical specialties, a number of units are designating/reorganising wards and theatres to serve subspecialty functions.

Example.

We reorganised what was a Maternity ward into areas which house colposcopy, laser and other treatments for cervical intraepithelial neoplasia; a urodynamic unit including an ultrasound facility; and an infertility unit. In each area provision has been made for private counselling as well as investigation; there are adequate waiting room and reception facilities.

Projects such as these need the help of the Estates Department. Staff, including planners, engineers, plumbers and so on, need to be brought together over a period of time to accomplish the task.

Summary

As doctor–manager in a clinical specialty you may have a large Directorate workforce, the salaries for which consume 75% of your budget. Managing a group of people of this size is difficult but vitally important.

A number of human resource management issues have been identified and discussed. Some of these are particularly relevant in the present time, e.g. recruitment and retention of staff are problems that are prevalent across all staff groups, medical and non-medical. Training of the different staff groups with regard to recent changes in NHS management is also identified as a major issue.

Motivating staff and maintaining job satisfaction are keys to success but hard to accomplish when the workforce is large and resources are limited.

Attention has been drawn to some difficulties relating to different staff groups: for doctors the problems associated with reduced hours of duty and training will figure high on your agenda; for nurses and midwives, recruitment and Project 2000 are serious issues; for non-medical staff, recruitment and job satisfaction will be hard to sustain if the workload continues to escalate.

Further reading

Department of Health and Social Security
1986 Hospital Medical Staffing: Achieving a Balance. HMSO, London

Department of Health and Social Security
1987 Hospital Medical Staffing: Achieving a Balance — Plan for Action. HMSO, London

Department of Health and Social Security
1990 Ministerial Group on Junior Doctors Hours. Heads of Agreement. HMSO, London

Department of Health and Social Security
1991 Junior Doctors — The New Deal. Hours of work of doctors in training: working arrangements for doctors and dentists in training. NHSME, London

National Health Service Management Executive
1991 Junior Doctors' Hours: The New Deal. Doctors in Training Documents. NHSME, London

6 Managing change

Introduction

"There is nothing more difficult, more perilous to conduct, or more uncertain in its success, than to take the lead in a new order of things, because the innovator has for enemies all those who have done well under the old conditions, and lukewarm defenders in those who may do well under the new. This coolness arises......partly from the fear of men, who do not readily believe in new things until they have experience of them."

(Machiavelli, 1469–1527)

If there is one thing you have to learn as a doctor–manager it is the management of change. The world is continuously undergoing change as are the organisations in it. The NHS is no exception. Due to many things, including shifts in strategic orientation away from technology-driven to market-driven services, the management of change has become a central feature on the agenda of any executive manager. It is not easy to respond and adapt to outside forces, not least because of the dilemma of maintaining stability in an organisation at the same time as being innovative.

Speed of change in the NHS

Change in the NHS is happening at a phenomenal rate. 'Even the future ain't what it was' is an extremely apposite quotation taken from Beckhard & Harris (1987), who begin by describing the speed of change. Some examples have been referred to already, namely Griffiths devolving management responsibility to clinicians; the NHS reforms introducing the concept of purchaser/provider; the whole shift of 'power' from hospital to GP through the implementation of GP fundholding; change in expectations of patients and staff such as the New Deal for Junior Doctors and the Patients' Charter.

Hospitals and their staff also have to cope with the rapid changes in patient management — particularly in the surgical specialties where there is minimally invasive surgery, laparoscopic work, the move towards surgery being performed on an outpatient basis and the rapid expansion of day case surgery.

Example.

In our Trust there were rapid changes secondary to a geographical relocation of some specialties. There was a need to rationalise services between two sister hospitals 4 miles apart. Some specialists had to start working on two sites; others shifted from traditional 'safe' environments to new, unfamiliar ones. The ratio of emergency to cold admissions at one of the hospitals was suddenly increased and at the other was as suddenly decreased. One outcome of this was a serious knock-on effect on other specialties at the 'acute' hospital. The bed crisis in the winter months was suddenly aggravated by the rationalisation policy — the influx of many more medical emergencies than usual jeopardised the function (and waiting-list status) of the surgical specialties.

Example.

Another change linked to the one above, arises from the New Deal for junior doctors. Quite reasonably, they are no longer expected to search for emergency beds in the hospital at night; so there has to be a bed-management team who have sufficient authority to overrule any attempt at bed-blocking or the operation of a hot-bed policy, whilst respecting the vulnerability of the smaller surgical specialties (such as gynaecology and ENT) whose function can be totally swamped by medical admissions.

Many changes in the NHS are happening at once and some of them are complex. If you are to survive in the environment from which the above examples are drawn, you must understand the change process and how to manage change. If it is ignored, the future never arrives — the present always wins. Things don't get better; they often get worse, so the present demands more attention than it deserves and the organisation spirals downwards.

The change process is inevitable and affects other organisations as well as the NHS, although perhaps the latter is moving more quickly now because it was slow to respond at the start. It has been said that the reforms recommended by Griffiths were slow to be implemented because at the time the NHS was so preoccupied with bureaucratic concerns (Turrell 1986). This is unfortunate because change should be spread over the longest possible time consistent with change requirements.

Organisational framework for change

Bureaucracy has been the traditional organisational framework of the NHS since its inception, but it is not innovative enough to meet the challenge of today's rapid change. It may be argued that some hospitals are mature organisations delivering a constant repertoire of behaviour efficiently and effectively and therefore bureaucracy suits them. But it is likely that financial pressures will lead them to explore ways of being more responsive, more efficient, more cost-effective, decentralised and able to handle the explosion of information technology, and they will have to change. Bureaucracies cannot handle change — an effective bureaucracy requires the world to be predictable and it is not.

The NHS has been a formal organisation with a strong emphasis on structure. In such an organisation logic rules, policies are debated and plans are made in orderly cycles and precede implementation. Rational bids are made for resources; performance measurement and control mechanisms are uniform so that they can be compared centrally. Communications are written. Reward is promotion. The organisation values certainty and has difficulty tolerating ambiguity.

There is immense change being imposed upon and expected from the NHS at the present time. It has difficulty responding satisfactorily because it remains very much a bureaucratic organisation (Fig. 6.1).

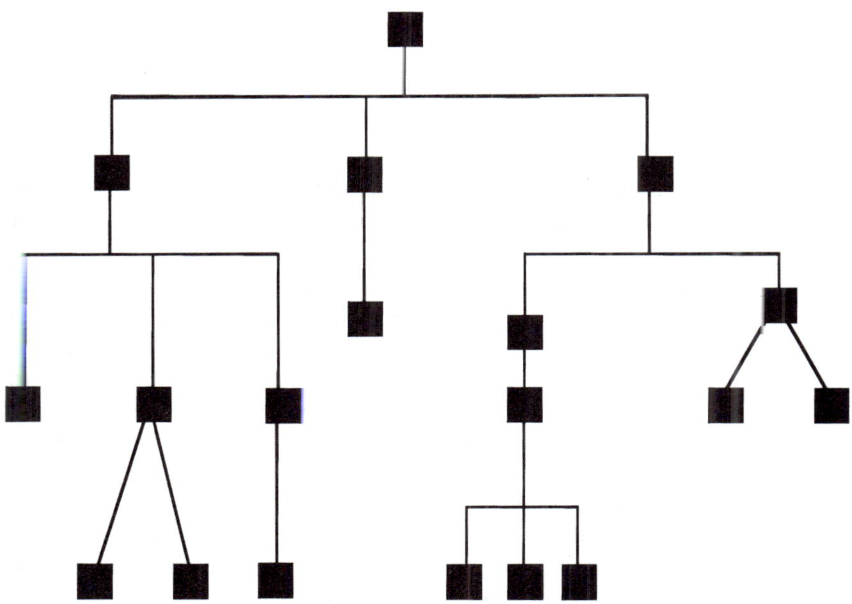

Figure 6.1 Bureaucracy structure

This description of the NHS is less applicable since the advent of resource management and the NHS reforms. New Directorates and similar bodies encourage more of a collegiate, innovative approach to patient care. The differences between innovative and non-innovative organisations are shown in Table 6.1 (Turrell 1986).

Table 6.1 Innovative vs non-innovative organisations

Innovative	Non-innovative
Change is normal	Change is shock
Organisation is collegiate	Organisation is bureaucratic, at least in part
Free flow of information	Constrained flow of information
Numerous horizontal connections	Vertical communication
Clear set of cultural beliefs	Idiosyncratic
Pride in the organisation	Uncertainty, confusion
Abundant rewards	Grudging rewards

Infant organisations are often *autocratic*: they have no need for a formal structure (Fig. 6.2). The focus is on the boss and his/her values. Such organisations can be innovative provided they remain small enough for the communication network to be maintained.

Anarchic organisations (Fig. 6.3) are ones in which people work but do so for themselves (e.g. self-employed consultancies). There is no common goal. Individuality is the key, standards are set professionally, reward is from job satisfaction and by recognition from peers. Some aspects of anarchical behaviour (the individuality and innovation) are useful in an organisation, but the cash-limited NHS has to have team spirit and a common goal.

In *collegiate* organisations (Fig. 6.4) individuals work for a significant part of their time in teams, based around particular tasks. Teams may have no long-term existence, and exist only for that task, then dispersing. So one individual may have several bosses. The individual is valued most for his/her competence, and achievement is his/her main reward.

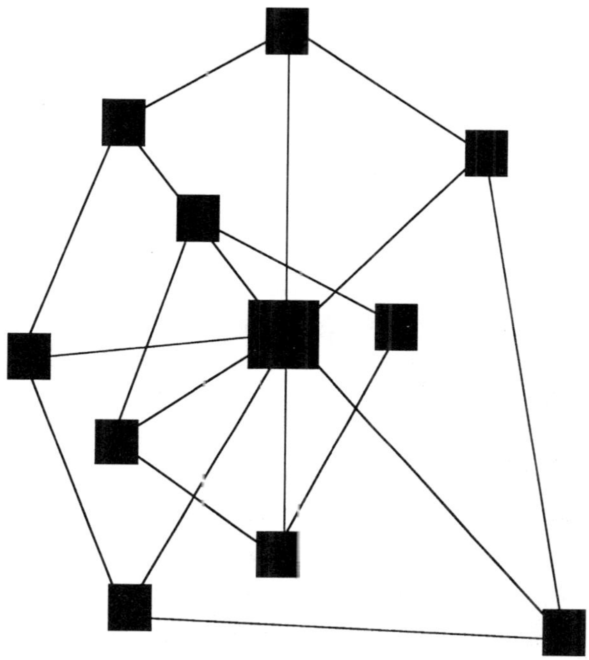

Figure 6.2 Autocratic structure

These organisations value variety and change. Decision-making is typically participative, ideas flow up and down.

It may be possible to build collegiate-like innovation into bureaucracies without necessarily destroying them (Turrell 1986). This would seem to be the way forward and the way to facilitate change management in the NHS.

Management of change

Change requires work and needs resources. You should manage the introduction of a different organisation as you would anything else — nominate change managers and allocate time and money.

Change is resource intensive even at Directorate level. Making a change always costs the individual and the organisation something — which may be money, resources, time or psychological demands. The latter is another reason why individuals resist change. You need to ensure that the cost is less than an individual's satisfaction.

Figure 6.3 Anarchic structure

The change equation

Change will be resisted unless:
A+B+C>D
where:
A = dissatisfaction with the present state;
B = vision of a better future;
C = acceptable first step;
D = cost to the individual of making the change.

The change process

Change is getting from the present state (which may be the 'steady-state' bureaucracy where your organisation stands at the present) to the future

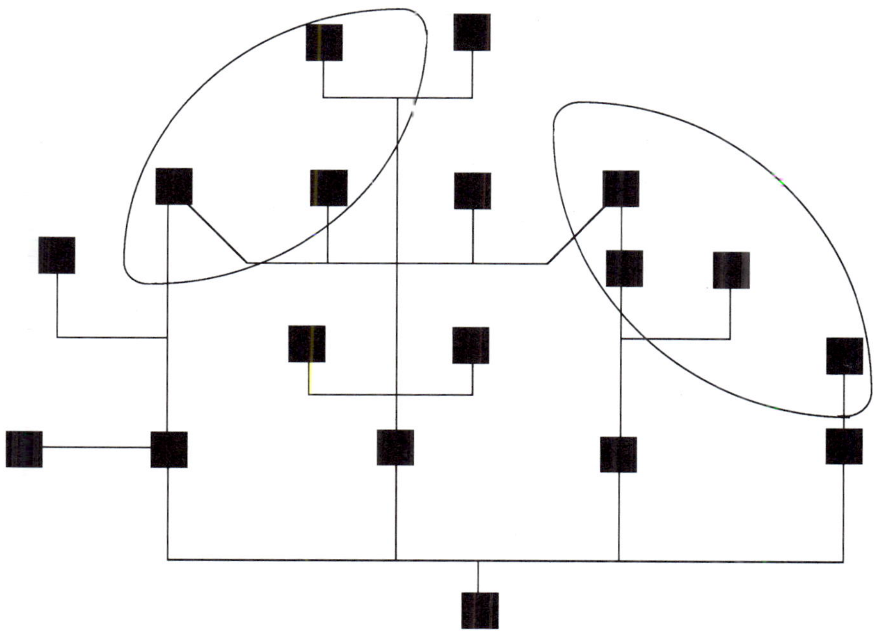

Figure 6.4 Collegiate structure

state (which is the position you wish to be in order to adapt to the changing internal and external environments). In between is the transition state. Each of these states demands management, careful planning and resource. The change process is not simply devising a strategy, it is also making plans and implementing them. There are difficulties associated with this. It assumes that reasonable people will do reasonable things and that existing systems and procedures will work for the new strategy. They do not. Also, it cannot be assumed that opposition can be overcome by use of authority, which it cannot. You have to use the change equation — in particular by providing a vision of a future which is better than the present and by overcoming the first hurdle towards it.

Successful change programmes are complex and incorporate innovation, leadership and opportunity. The innovative organisation builds in change as a norm, encouraging individuals to behave entrepreneurially. A map of the change management process is shown in Figure 6.5.

The need for change

The most crucial point is *establishing the need* for change. You will have

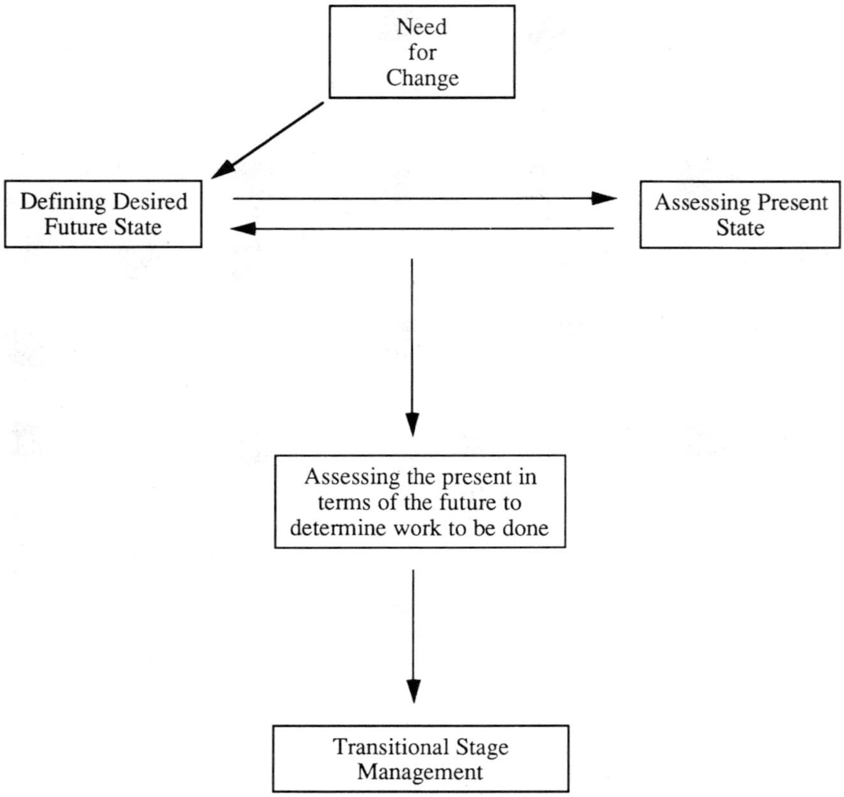

Figure 6.5 Map of the change management process

a hard time after the event convincing people that change was necessary if you did not work out the pros and cons for it first. So the need for change has to be established — and *accepted*. Unfortunately, in the NHS, change has happened so fast that it has been almost impossible to understand the need yourself, let alone sell it to the workforce.

Defining the need for change means locating the sources of pressure for change, identifying those that are external and those that are internal and which you think should be targetted. For large systems such as the NHS most of the pressures originate externally. The most obvious ones were described in Chapter 1, e.g. the NHS reforms; but there are other more subtle changes such as a greater understanding by patients of medical disorders and hence greater expectations of cure; a greater inclination towards litigation if things go wrong; and a greater wish by patients to be *involved* in the treatment process and decisions regarding treatment.

As far as the external forces are concerned there is no question of *whether* you should respond or adapt to them, but rather *how* you should do so. In these situations the members of the leadership team have no choice but to anticipate the demand for change.

At other times the forces for change are clearly internal and, given the appropriate resource, you, as change leader, have the option of deciding both whether and how to start the change process.

> **Example.**
>
> In our O&G Directorate there was a need to develop subspecialty facilities in urogynaecology, colposcopy and infertility investigation. All were previously accommodated in small, inadequate rooms where there was no changing facility, no privacy, no storage space, etc. The need for change was clear. What was also clear was the present situation, the desired future state, and the transitional management needed to reach that end point.

Sometimes the perceived need for change is not so clear — or the internal or external forces are interpreted differently by different members of the team.

> **Example.**
>
> In Midwifery there is a national groundswell of opinion against high-tech, doctor-based maternity care for low-risk pregnancies. There has always been intense debate over what constitutes a low-risk pregnancy because it can only be recognised in retrospect. It is also understood that high-technology intrapartum care over the last two decades will have saved many babies' lives. Nonetheless, women want less intervention, more midwife-managed care and more personal involvement with their management. It was our view that we had to respond to this force, and we implemented a high-risk/low-risk policy for maternity care, with obstetric surveillance.

Defining the future state

There must be an overall objective, a core mission, a vision of the future. This is different from organisational objectives or goals: the core mission is the organisation's *raison d'etre*. There may be several mid-point objectives but they have to be prioritised if the organisation is to be purposeful. For example, you may want to develop a section of your service which is deficient at the moment; or you may wish to introduce a new system of management for a particular group of patients. A number of objectives or goals should be defined and encompassed in your overall core mission. However, there has to be one overriding *core purpose* which will guide management and set priorities/allocate resources.

The core mission/purpose

In the NHS, the mission of a DGH might be one or more of the following:

- a place where sick people are cured;
- an institution for developing new treatments;
- a training institution for junior doctors and nurses;
- a research institute;
- an interesting place to work;
- a centre for the promotion of health, e.g. preventative medicine;
- a centre of excellence providing care which cannot be provided elsewhere;
- a centre where resources are used to the best effect for achieving any of the above.

This is one of the dilemmas you will face, because you may want the hospital or Directorate to be all of these things and this is not possible within your remit. Or you may have a particular interest in research or, say, preventative medicine. If you are to succeed in the role as change manager all your clinical colleagues must be pointing in the same direction, with one common vision of the future, one common mission.

Mid-point goals

There is also a belief that clarity of mission alone does not mobilise sufficient energy to make the change happen, and it may be more appropriate to identify one or more *mid-point goals*. These should be at a specific time far enough into the future to provide a sense of the feasibility of the projected changes. These future states bear in mind the core mission in the same way as does the *end point*.

> **Example.**
>
> In our hospital O&G services were provided at opposite ends of the campus. We would like to see the development of a 'Women's Hospital' on the site of the present Maternity unit, thereby amalgamating the two halves of the specialty. This is our vision of the future but it is at present unattainable because of lack of resource. Instead we have achieved something of a mid-point goal by transferring subspecialty gynaecology, gynaecology outpatients and gynaecology records to the Maternity block, and have built an 'Early Pregnancy Disorders' unit onto an existing Antenatal Assessment Unit.

Assessing the present state

You need to know where you stand at the present in order to determine what is needed for the transition phase, i.e. what needs to be changed. In large organisations it may be appropriate to bring in a team of management consultants to study the organisation objectively. Within a Clinical Directorate (or its equivalent) the convening of working parties is usually sufficient to establish what is the present situation. These can then report, for discussion, to the Directorate forum itself.

Where facilities are very poor, assessment of the present is easy. At other times there is a danger that focusing on problems identified in the present may magnify negative experiences and the possibility of failure. Creativity in goal setting and problem solving may be stifled by fears of impracticability. So sometimes you have momentarily to ignore the present and concentrate on the future.

In general, however, the two pictures of the desired future state and the present state (defined in that order) determine the work which needs to be done in the transition phase.

Managing the transition stage

In practice, the strategy setting and planning processes take time and induce suspicion in those not involved. This produces maximum resistance. There is often little opportunity to generate the commitment which would result from involvement in decision making or for organisational learning. Compliance is sought by negotiation, manipulation, persuasion, barter or naked power pressure. You must not let delay set in because this is often fatal.

> **Example.**
>
> In Gynaecology there is uncertainty about the funding of assisted conception (IVF, etc.). It is expensive and so the view is held by some that it should only be provided in the private sector. Assessment of the present situation indicates that, not only is the funding of IVF an impossibility, but the capping of drug expenditure on conventional ovulation stimulation severely curtails this programme. The present situation is that we provide a poor service. What needs to be done for the transition phase is to identify resources (e.g. pharmaceutical companies, links with the private sector, transfer IVF techniques) such that a business plan can be developed and presented to the purchaser.

Sometimes luck plays a part in the change programme and an unexpected external event helps the situation.

> **Example.**
>
> In this Trust, the unexpected influx of extra EFL (External Financing Limit) money at the beginning of a financial year allowed certain long-hoped-for building projects to be started. These included the development of a new Postgraduate Teaching Unit and enhancement of the hospital foyer such that it incorporated shops (and so generates further income).

If a change leader can seize upon opportunities such as this to start the change process, it may move smoothly, particularly if it is possible to share the strategy with key personnel to drive the change along.

The more complex approach whereby the combination of many factors including innovation, leadership and opportunistic strategy supercedes the simple strategy/plan/implementation cycle tends to build on a number of small projects rather than large ones (which induce resistance), though there has to be overall direction to ensure that the organisation's core purpose is achieved. At the end of the process the different behaviours become institutionalised and lasting (until the next change).

Key dilemmas of the change process

Turrell (1986) described the key dilemmas of the change process, namely:

1. *Simple beliefs vs complex issues.* As doctor–manager you will be inundated most of the time with troubleshooting problems (see Chapter 2). The dilemma is how to keep the principles in view whilst dealing with this detail.

2. *A need for experimentation vs a need to be right.* One of the characteristics of change is that it generates conflict and polarises opinions. Medical and nursing staff are rarely entrepreneurial: the whole of their training is contradictory to this. They are taught not to accept any new investigation method or treatment modality unless it has been proven by scientific study. But a doctor–manager in the new organisation has to adopt some entrepreneurial attitudes in order to manage the change process — and you have to gain the support of clinical colleagues and carry them with you. There will be inevitable conflict and differing opinions between 'steady state' staff and those enthusiastic about moving forwards — particularly if the current state is comfortable (the so-called fat cat syndrome).

3. *People tend to think of change as being top-driven,* imposed from above. Harvey-Jones (1988) admits that until he was senior enough in ICI to pull levers nothing changed. So there does need to be powerful leadership from the top but in hospitals, as in other organisations, the dilemma lies in achieving overall top direction whilst encouraging change at 'shop floor' level — where change really happens. In the NHS, the patient is at ground level and so worthwhile change in patient management must be implemented by staff working at this level who are sufficiently motivated and committed (and who have sufficient strength) to implement change. So there needs to be *powerful leadership and empowered followers*: direction is needed at senior level, but the actual change process should happen at ground level.

4. *Managing the present vs managing change.* It has been stated already that each stage in the change process requires management, resources and effort. The present state might be a bureaucracy in which you are trying to introduce innovation, but it still needs management and resource. The transition phase is an activity in its own right; if ignored the future will simply not arrive. Finally, projected resources have to be allocated to the changed situation once it has been reached. Another dilemma is maintaining a bureaucracy (which may be delivering the goods at the right place, the right time and at the right quality according to static, 'best procedure' rules and guidelines) whilst encouraging innovation in the future and in the management of the transition phase (which may be something of a gamble).

5. *External and internal environmental changes* will exert demands on the organisation and expect new responses from it.

External factors which have complicated the programme of change in most Directorates (other than Government philosophy) include:

- the need to reduce junior doctors' hours of duty;
- the explosion in information technology;

- purchaser/provider shift;
- GP fundholding;
- fall in nurse recruitment; Project 2000.

Internal changes are supposed to be less of a problem because they are under your control — at least in part, although many of the so-called internal changes in the NHS are, in fact, imposed. Internal changes which have been particularly influencial include:

- Changes in the nursing hierarchy. This has been described earlier: the fact that senior nurses are part of the Directorate system and are now accountable in managerial issues to you, rather than to the Head Nurse, adds a new dimension to change management.
- Information technology inside the hospital might seem to be within your control but it is not. The benefits of a multimillion pound investment in IT have not yet been realised and so it is difficult to keep this particular 'mission' alive in the minds of colleagues and the workforce.

Overcoming resistance to change

There may be excitement, 'buzz', amongst those involved with the change process and those who can implement it, but disfavour amongst those who are not. The involvement of staff with the change process is an important motivator (empowered followers).

Force field analysis

Not every change inside or outside your organisation is going to make you change your plans. There are restraining forces as well as driving forces in both arenas, hence the '*force field*' analogy. An organisation is kept in balance by the interaction of two opposing sets of forces — those that seek to promote change, or *driving forces* and those that seek to maintain the status quo, or *restraining forces* (Fig. 6.6).

Resistance to change

A characteristic of change is its uncertainty. Individuals often resist change because of fear of the unknown. They can manage the way things are but not the uncertainties of the future.

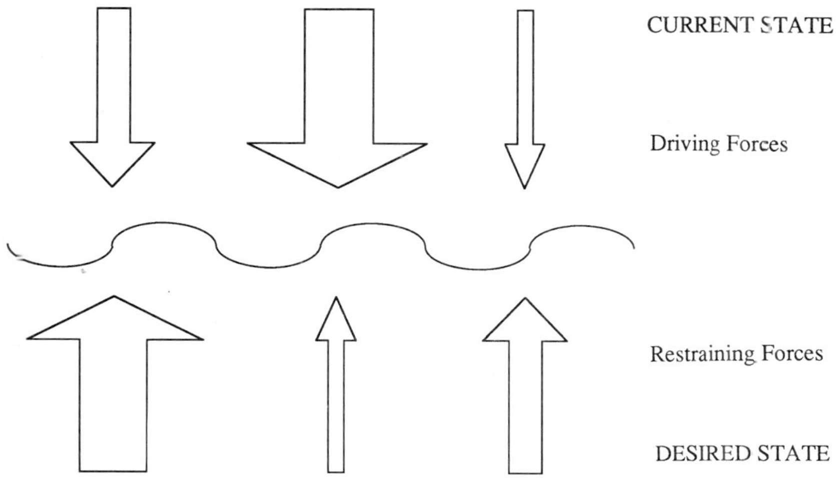

Figure 6.6 Force field analysis

Turrell (1986) lists the excuses made to avoid change: we have all made them or have heard them often enough in the NHS from colleagues who are resistant to change:

- it isn't the right time;
- we don't have the right resources;
- the circumstances will be better next week, month, year;
- it is too soon after the last one;
- we need more data;
- we really need to convene a multidisciplinary working party to look into it;
- we don't want change for change's sake;
- we need evolution not revolution;
- we must wait until . . . everyone is in post, the structures have been agreed, the Government changes, the committee reports . . . etc.

Hard and soft options

Some problems are easily soluble — like a simple mathematics problem; others by asking someone to do it for you; others only by making educated guesses. The difference between (easy) uncomplicated mathematical solutions to a problem and the solutions which take into account people variations, i.e. those which need educated guesses, are the hard and soft problems — the soft having no single or simple solution (Table 7.2). In general, the more intractable change problems are at the 'soft' end of the spectrum.

Table 7.2 Differences between hard and soft problems

Hard	Soft
One clear solution	No clear solution
Solution can be only one thing	Resolution can be one of many things
Know what the problem is	Not sure what the problem is
Know what needs to be known	Not sure what needs to be known
Clear methods for working it out	No obvious method for working it out
Structured	Unstructured
Clear-cut	Messy

Some aspects of change can be described as being 'messy'. In these there are no 'boundaries' to the problem and you cannot get a good grasp of the situation. With a 'bounded', well-defined problem there may be, e.g.

- a limited timescale;
- clear priorities;
- a limited number of people involved;
- knowledge of what the problem is and what needs to be known
- a solution

This compares with a messy, unbounded problem, where there is likely to be, e.g.:

- an uncertain timescale;

- questionable priorities;
- uncertain implications;
- more people involved;
- lack of clarity about what the problem is or what needs to be known;
- no clear solutions.

Some of the problems associated with change management come into the 'soft' category; they are 'messy', and have no clear solution. An attempt to treat an ill-defined problem as a straightforward difficulty involves neglecting certain aspects....it then becomes poorly defined and unbounded. By now you have wasted time, aggravated people, reduced productivity and lost credibility. Cautious analysis of a problem in the early stages is essential.

Summary

In a healthy innovative organisation there is an equilibrium between a number of elements:

- *The formal organisational arrangements* can be written down on paper: they include lines of accountability, budgets, formal meeting and committee structures, job descriptions, terms and conditions of service, pay and reward procedures, information systems, monitoring and control mechanisms. These arrangements are devised to meet the needs of the organisation as it was yesterday and are unlikely to match the needs of tomorrow. At times of change the formal organisation focuses on authority.
- *The informal organisation* is less tangible. It includes the culture, the major values of the organisation (e.g. quality assurance); and also rites and rituals, the human aspects of the organisation, who you know, string-pulling, horse trading, allegiencies, alliancies, professionalism, loyalties, etc. (see Turrell 1986). At times of change the informal organisation focuses on power.
- *Individuals* come and go bringing different skills and attitudes. The formal organisation assumes that people can be matched to a job but in practice no two people tackle the same job in the same way. Some will adapt the structure to meet their personal needs.
- *Tasks*. The organisation exists in order to pursue some purposeful human activity, so the tasks are the prime reason for the organisation to exist.

If the organisation is healthy, as one element changes the others shift to accommodate. Change leaders need to work with all four elements if they are to succeed. The NHS may have concentrated too much on the formal procedures in the past.

The arguments for organisational change have been presented with the concluding view that there should be a shift away from pure bureaucracy towards a more collegiate system. So part of your role as doctor–manager/change leader is to study organisational choices and move your part of the NHS in that direction.

The elements of the change process are:

- clarity of core purpose;
- shared vision of a better future;
- operating principles;
- environmental constraints;
- transition management;
- resistance reduction;
- commitment planning.

There are a number of requirements to be met and dilemmas to be solved for a successful change programme to take place. An important element at the start is an agreed understanding of the purpose of the enterprise. The organisation must have a core purpose; there needs to be a clear vision of the desired future, what the organisation is aiming at. Next, this must be compared with the present in order to define the transition needed. The transition stages must be thought out carefully (without losing the entrepreneurial spirit) because they are subject to a host of external and internal environmental pressures. Resources, time and effort must be devoted to each stage of the process and overall leadership must be provided throughout.

Further reading

Beckhard R, Harris R T
1987 Organisational Transitions, Organisation Development Series. Managing Complex Change. 2nd edn Addison-Wesley Publishing, Wokingham

Harvey-Jones J
1986 Making it Happen. Reflections on Leadership. Fontana, London

Turrell E A
1986 Change and Innovation: A Challenge for the NHS. The Institute of Health Service Management, London

7 Ongoing change: The future

Introduction

This chapter is intended to draw attention to some of the ongoing changes that are happening in the NHS, to some of the difficulties that you might have to face in the future if you take on a managerial role, and to some of the anxieties clinicians have about the present system.

First it should be appreciated that the new system following the reforms is still young and developing. Many lessons have still to be learned. Some centres are way ahead of others in their exposure to the new systems. As mentioned in this book's preface, Clinical Directorates followed Trust status in some hospitals; in others they followed in the wake of Clinical Information Systems. Our own experience is from a RMI pilot site. Therefore, there will be different levels of understanding and appreciation of the benefits and disadvantages of the new order across the country, and the perception of how the reforms are working will vary greatly.

The review by Abel-Smith (1993) of the first 2 years of NHS reforms emphasises that they have not yet really started to bite: hospitals, as provider units have not yet got their teeth into realistic costing; and the budgets of GPs and DHAs as purchasing units are likely to become increasingly tight.

It is our view that the reforms have many commendable features. Being a clinician in charge of the future of your Department is immensely satisfying. Even with limited resources you are in a position to prioritise developments in your specialty — this has never happened before in the NHS. You have a finger on the pulse of your Department, rather than having only an insular view of your own firm. You do get to know all the staff, all the problems facing different sections of the Department and how to help overcome them. This close involvement and ability to influence the direction in which you are heading is hugely rewarding and will give you great satisfaction. You are also involved in formulating hospital policy and can play some part in deciding the direction in which the hospital moves.

However, there are many issues that are contentious and many problems still to be overcome if the new reforms are to work. We discuss these concerns in the final chapter in as critical a way as possible in order to make clear the changes that you will have to face in the next few years. The clock cannot be turned back: Trusts, Clinical Directorates and doctors in management are here to stay.

If you are about to undertake a management role we hope that being aware of some of the potential threats will equip you better to deal with them, and to fight your corner. Whilst a corporate view has to be maintained, the essence of your job as doctor–manager is to look after your patch, manage your budget and care for the needs of your patients and staff.

GP fundholding

The intention behind the introduction of GP fundholding was to bring GPs and hospital consultants together in the provision and management of both primary and secondary health care. The clinical power switch from hospital to GP is creating immense tensions. Hospital consultants who have spent years in the training grades on specialist career ladders find it hard to accept that they are *providers* of a service.

Some feel that they have no input into patient management. Worse than that, they are having to jump when a GP says jump. If they don't, the business goes elsewhere and jobs are lost. The only way around some of these potential 'power relationship' problems is to work more closely and in partnership with GPs.

By 1995 it is estimated that 75% of all patients will be registered with GP fundholding practices. So, it could be that very soon nearly all elective surgical procedures will be determined by GPs.

The four main areas of a GP budget that impact most on hospital practice can be identified as:

- outpatient work;
- elective surgery;
- diagnostic services;
- domiciliaries.

Outpatient work

Referral to the private sector. In parts of the country there has already been a change in referral patterns away from NHS hospitals to the private sector. An NHS clinic visit costs a GP about £40, but with this goes all the aggravation for the patient: waiting for an appointment; waiting a long time in clinic; not necessarily seeing the consultant; being allowed only a short time for the actual consultation. For £20 or so more the GP can refer patients for a private consultation and guarantee *quality* for the patient. There is evidence that GP fundholders are not going for cheapness but for quality.

Referral pattern change within the NHS. Rather than send patients for private consultations some GP fundholders have arranged for consultants to do clinics in their practices. In some Districts, GP practices are organising themselves into groups (locality networks) so that sufficient patients can be gathered together to make a consultant visit cost effective. Such *peripheral clinics* can be arranged so that there is little waiting time for an appointment, the patient is seen in a friendly environment and there is no wait in the clinic. Practice nurses can be trained to provide support and organise the practice functions and may even become partners in the practice (Dyson, personal communication).

There should be no criticism of GPs because the evidence is that they simply want the facility to expose patients more directly to consultants, to work in partnership with consultants and to learn from them. But there is no doubt that any consultant who behaves in any way superior to GP colleagues will lose business (and perhaps that of colleagues and the hospital).

Referral elsewhere in the NHS. If a high quality service is provided elsewhere in the NHS and is less expensive as well, the GP fundholder may send patients to that unit regardless of the distance.

Example.

An ophthalmology service in one part of the country was able to draw in patients from surrounding Regions for cataract removal. In the competing units the costs for this treatment were about three times as high, so they lost the business.

The effect of these changing patterns of outpatient care may be the need to reduce staffing levels in NHS hospitals.

Elective surgery

Patients do not like to stay in hospital unless it is absolutely necessary. A major increase in day-case surgery is predicted (our own Unit's day case work increased by 125% in 1991/1992). Across the country, the percentage day-case figure is likely to exceed 50% of all surgical work. The knock-on effect of day-case surgery is that patients are more likely to have all their preoperative workup and follow up in their general practice; this again reducing the need for hospital nursing staff. The hospital bed-base will have to contract.

> **Example.**
>
> Day-case hernias. Provided a GP is licensed (i.e. trained) to deal with hernias, the consultant may only get to see the patient when he/she arrives on the operating table: everything else, before and after, is done by the GP. It is apparently extremely cost effective and safe and the number of patients in whom the diagnosis is wrong is small (estimated at 3%).

Diagnostic services

GPs are already organising their own pathology and radiology services. Some of these are via independent private units — which may have more support staff than the NHS and which may be able to pay them better. In other cases, GPs are buying in X-ray, ultrasound and colposcopy apparatus to be used on their practice premises.

Domiciliaries

Presumably there will be less need for domiciliaries if consultants visit GP practices regularly, or if clinics are established closer to patients' homes. Often domiciliary visits are requested in order to provide advice: the closer collaboration between GP and hospital doctor should make most of these unnecessary.

Benefits from fundholding

Some major benefits have arisen form the introduction of GP fundholding. The enthusiasm of fundholders and potential fundholders for providing a better quality service has caused them to extract more from the hospital unit. Situations that used to anger them are now suddenly up for negotiation (Roland 1991). For example:

- Why should patients wait weeks to hear about their appointments?
- Why should patients wait months to see the specialist?
- Why should patients wait hours in outpatient clinics before being seen?

Fundholding has caused these issues to be tackled and has opened up a completely new dialogue between primary and secondary care. Whether or not the questions can be answered is a different issue.

GPs are well able to argue the case for better services for their patients (although not necessarily for the whole population). They are often entrepreneurial (particularly the early wave fundholders), and good at responding to the demands of their individual patients. They have the advantage of knowing their small population intimately and where they might be best treated. Of course, this does not add up to a health strategy for the whole population. Health Authorities, with larger populations to consider, do not understand, nor can they predict, individual needs so accurately but they should be in a better position to give a global view.

The practice-based innovations are important also, although they are not unique to fundholding practices. Many practices have developed generic prescribing policies, computerised information systems, specialist clinics, minor surgery sessions, diagnostic facilities and protocols for shared care.

Hospital doctors seem now to be keen to develop better rapport with GPs, and not simply to keep their business. It seems there had always been a deficiency in this interface and the NHS reforms have acted as something of a catalyst in bringing the two groups together.

Example.

At one of the first meetings convened by a Directorate to discuss respective business plans with a group of potential GP fundholders, a senior GP remarked afterwards that this was the first time in his long experience (since the NHS started) that this sort of discourse had been possible.

GPs and hospital doctors are now collaborating in the production of joint protocols for the management of common conditions (e.g. hypertension, diabetes, menorrhagia) so that investigations are not duplicated; the patient has no unnecessary visits to hospital; and follow-up guidelines enable some care previously undertaken by the hospital to be done by GPs, etc. All of this should smooth the patient's progress through the investigation, treatment and follow-up stages of the illness. The 'working together' of primary health care and hospital groups in order to provide a better deal for patients should be satisfying for all concerned.

Anxieties about fundholding

Two-tier medical care

There is no doubt that, at present, there is a *two tier provision* of medical care. Because of the pressures GPs are able to put on a hospital's administrative staff (i.e. Chief Executive and deputies), some can secure contracts that give advantage to their patients over others. If the NHS is to be run in line with regular business methods, contracts have to be won and honoured. If a contract is not fulfilled the hospital (and its staff) will suffer.

It is easy to see how a two-tier system of patient care can develop almost by default. Some degree of preferential treatment for patients on fundholders' lists is inevitable. The GPs who were keen enough to be first- and second-wave fundholders have 'blazed the trail' — in establishing peripheral clinics, for example. Patients attending such clinics are seen sooner than those coming to hospital and, if inpatient treatment is necessary, they are added to the waiting list sooner.

Fundholders are driving the internal market and, because they have addressed quality of care in setting contracts, it is inevitable that a two-tier standard of care will develop. Indeed, this must happen if the plan is to work, i.e. to act as a lever to produce change across the whole NHS (Roland 1991).

Example.

An Orthopaedic Directorate considered it not to be cost-effective for the population as a whole to deploy senior staff to run a peripheral GP clinic. As a result almost the whole of the orthopaedic referrals from that practice now go to a neighbouring District.

Presumably, however, when all GPs become fundholders (if they do.... there is some evidence that some may opt out, and many are still opposed to it), (a) it will no longer be possible to staff so many peripheral clinics, and (b) other means of making the service more localised will have to be devised.

Effect of peripheral clinics on hospital units

There are knock-on effects of locality/peripheral clinics that have not yet been appreciated. It is tempting to believe that consultant clinics held on a regular basis in GP practices (or in locality clinics, or in previously closed hospital units) will be good for patients and will bring in extra business for the hospital unit. These clinics will allow closer contact (for those patients attending) with the secondary care doctor. As a hospital consultant, you will enjoy doing them; they take you away from the hospital environment for a time and allow you to look at things from a different perspective. But you cannot be expected to take on extra outpatient work without cancelling existing clinics. The number of patients you are able to see in a locality clinic is likely to be far fewer than in your hospital clinic. Furthermore, you will not be able to supervise junior staff, teach (postgraduates and undergraduates) or cover other hospital duties. The knock-on effect on patients referred from non-fundholding practices may be serious.

As a consultant, your presence speeds up a clinic and allows more patients to be seen. It promotes a greater throughput. Presumably, some clinics will have to proceed without immediate consultant cover — but this breaks the Patients' Charter. At best, difficult cases which a registrar cannot handle will need to be brought back for another consultation when the consultant is present and this will reduce the time available for new patients.

So, as a doctor–manager, how do you choose? If you go for the peripheral clinics you may bring in some extra business from a few practices; but you will exacerbate the pressures on your central unit. You may then be unable to fulfil undergraduate and postgraduate junior staff teaching commitments (which themselves will soon be market driven), and so you may lose medical staff. Patients may have to wait longer in your base clinic or have to return for your advice to another clinic — so the referring GP may send them elsewhere and you will have the Chief Executive on your back for not maintaining activity (with the threat that some of your non-medical staff will be lost). This is a no-win situation for everybody.

In these situations compromises have to be made for the benefit of the patient and service. As doctor–manager you will have to explore ways of doing this. You may be able to deploy senior staff (e.g. Associate Specialists) to GP/locality clinics; you may be able to delegate teaching to specific 'senior' members of your team.

Pacing of referrals

The Government has already put a cash limit on prescribing. The fundholding scheme may have been designed to see whether it is possible to do the same with referrals. The Secretary of State for Health has advised her senior managers to encourage the pacing of referrals so that contracts do not expire before year end. To add to the confusion, a recent directive from the NHSME was that 'urgent' patients should still be seen and treated after a contract had been fulfilled because "it is simply unacceptable to offer significantly different standards of care to this group of patients, depending on the time in the financial year at which they present". But who decides which patients are urgent and for whom the contract should be broken?

Tight GP budgets

Another difficulty may arise when all GPs become fundholders and their budgets became increasingly tight. There is evidence that many of the early fundholders were overfunded — certainly there was wide variation in budgets allocated to first-wave fundholders (Day & Klein 1991), but with limited overall resource there may be insufficient money to finance the last wave. The savings that the first-wave fundholders were able to achieve will not be possible again and the question of how to fund the remaining fundholders at the end of the exercise (in 2–3 years) has not yet been addressed. Budgets will, by then, be tight and GPs will find themselves on the frontline of the rationing process. A worrying problem is that practices may be persuaded to indulge in '*cream skimming*', whereby patients with expensive health care needs are removed from GP lists (Weiner & Ferriss 1990), or, at least, not referred for secondary care. The crucial test of fundholding relates to the fixed budget. A constrained budget will prevent GPs from referring patients and underreferral will go unnoticed because it is hard to detect.

Purchaser choice

The fundholding system was intended to promote continuous service review as purchasers renegotiate service agreements in search of better value. It requires that purchasers make rational and informed choices between different providers, but this is not possible (Eve & Hodgkin 1991). Detailed cost analyses of services given by provider units are only just emerging, as are measures of patients' needs and clinical outcomes. These cannot be provided by DHAs because clinical outcomes occur in the community, not hospitals, so hospital data are of no use; and patients' needs rely on feedback from GPs, which is not measured.

Abuse of the system

Some practices have been allowed to establish private companies to enable them to sell and buy services from themselves, e.g. practices that have established services like physiotherapy dramatically increase their referral to these facilities. Is this demand induced by suppliers or abuse of the system? Preventing abuse will require careful regulation.

Clearly, there is a long way to go before the dust settles on the fundholding issue. In some instances, GPs appear to be flexing muscle and making inordinate demands on the hospital unit. One would hope that the blame for poor services (like waiting lists, etc.) is really being levelled at the lack of resources in the NHS as a whole, but the 'pig-in-the-middle' is the doctor who takes on a managerial role and the Service Manager, who are constantly hounded on one side by the Chief Executive to return better activity figures and reduce waiting times, and, indirectly, are threatened by GP colleagues that referrals may go elsewhere. For the hospital doctor engaged in management, it is difficult sometimes to see who your friends are.

Management changes

Generic Business Managers

In some long-standing Directorate hospitals there is a move to strengthen the position of the Business Manager by discarding the triumvirate system (described in Chapter 2), and replacing it with a Clinical Director/Business Manager partnership, with the Business Manager carrying responsibilities for more than one Directorate and being paid more.

In less successful Directorates, a more senior Business Manager (albeit having cross-Directorate duties) would provide greater support for the Clinical Director and, of course, would replace any weak managers. Poor Clinical Directors will be less easy to dislodge but the seniority of the generic Business Manager will overcome this problem.

There are obvious advantages to this new system, the main one being the proper recognition of the Business Manager's role. However, there are also some anxieties. As doctor–manager you will note that it generates a subtle shift back towards central management — away from the principles of resource management (where it was intended that management be devolved to its smallest possible denominator). It is inevitable that an elite group of senior 'executive' Business Managers will have stronger allegiance to the Chief Executive. So there is a serious concern amongst some medical personnel that the Clinical Director will become nothing more than a figure-head — being wheeled in and out to stamp documents. If the Business Manager has such a strong position, the Clinical Director's role may be diluted and devalued. The Chief Executive may argue that such high calibre staff will free-up creative time for the Clinical Directors and give them more time to devote to the unit's future, the hospital's future, and to liaise with GPs and purchasers, i.e. to give the Clinical Directors more time for a 'director' or leadership role. But there is a danger that we shall revert to pre-Griffiths' bureaucracy with doctors having little input.

It is important for you as doctor–manager to recognise some of these subtle changes. Close rapport with the Chief Executive via whom you can make your position clear is valuable. You will have to learn how to continue to be influential in a managerial system which may not like doctors to be influential. In contrast to your job as doctor, which is fairly safe, managerial and administrative jobs are not so secure. It is understandable that the Chief Executive will want a successful management structure in order to secure the position/tenure of Chief Executive staff, particularly if the devolution of managerial responsibility is to a group of doctors who cannot handle it. The onus is on medical staff to learn how to do it properly.

Where should change be happening?

Harvey-Jones' precept of a successful organisation being top-led but bottom-driven means that change happens at shop-floor level — and change costs money. Resource should be being injected at this level but this does not seem to be happening. As a doctor–manager you will need to fight for audit assistants, technical staff, ancillary staff, etc.

Enhanced role of Medical Director

An alternative way for doctors to retain a force in the post-reform NHS would be to introduce some hierarchy into their system. Perhaps there should be some sort of ranking whereby a Medical Director (on the Trust Board) can impose clinical restrictions upon colleagues if they do not conform or agree to agreed Directorate protocols and budgetary restrictions. This is a very sensitive issue which we raise for debate. There still appear to be many abusers of the system whereby doctors in management use the position to further their own particular goal; and others who achieve the same by having a loud voice.

Quality issues

Type of service provided

In Chapter 6 (under 'core-mission'), we described the difficulties in deciding what service you should provide: whether your unit should be a centre of excellence; one providing low-cost, high-quality care for the majority of the population; a teaching centre; a research institute, etc. In a recent lecture by a Chief Executive advocating 'Patient-Focused Care', it was admitted that his hospital had no aspirations other than to provide 'high quality care' for the majority of patients in the District served by the Trust. Many doctors would find this approach hard to accept, even in a DGH. They will want to excel, to provide a service better than anywhere else.

There are suggestions also that doctors in specialist training should be streamlined early in their careers (junior registrar stage) towards a future either in hospitals providing basic (high-quality) care or in centres of excellence. It is hard to imagine how such a crucial decision can be made so early in one's career and how much progress in medicine will be lost from losing the 'late developers' — and, indeed, how much frustration will be generated in those doctors programmed for a 'basic' career when they do develop a special interest.

Of course, it can be argued that some services should not be provided by all hospitals because they are expensive (see p. 169), and should instead be concentrated in specialist centres, i.e. some disorders should instead be referred to tertiary centres. There is kudos in being a tertiary referral centre and so hospital doctors will try to achieve this status in order to attract staff. This is not necessarily compatible with Central Management's view of high-throughput, low-cost care.

Example.

Assisted conception is an expensive service and perhaps should be provided only in Regional or SupraRegional Units. But one in six couples have some difficulty in conceiving. So to serve its population properly, should not every DGH have an assisted conception unit?

Quality

The current preoccupation with quality can be seen as being about value for money and may be part of the drive for economic efficiency. The distinction has to be recognised between commerce and public service. Quality approaches imported into the public services from the commercial world may fail because they do not acknowledge this.

There are innumerable training programmes claiming to teach people how to achieve quality; the Government announces new quality initiatives everywhere; the pursuit of quality is being heralded as the solution to many of the problems besetting the welfare state. But, although everyone seems to be talking about quality, its meaning changes according to context and the person using it. Different people experience it in different ways. For example, managers will use quality to describe throughput and patient satisfaction in pursuit of market advantage.

Doctors will perceive quality in a very different sense, e.g. conforming to standards determined by experts.

A further cause of confusion is that quality in health and social services is linked to fundamental changes in the politics and organisation of the welfare state — and therefore what it meant yesterday does not necessarily hold today.

Members of the public are increasingly concerned about falling standards of provision — on account of limited resources, rising demands, escalating costs and political limits on public expenditure. The invocation of quality is a sign that welfare providers and politicians are responding to these concerns. But it is not always simply about trying to improve services. Sometimes quality initiatives are used as a smoke-screen to mask the effects of intensifying pressures on resources (Pfeffer & Coote 1991).

Pfeffer & Coote (1991) identified five purposes for the use of the word quality, namely:

- to convey prestige and positional advantage (the traditional purpose);
- to conform to standards set by experts (the scientific purpose);
- to measure customer satisfaction in pursuit of market advantage (the managerial approach);
- to empower the customer (the consumerist approach);
- to achieve common goals in the interests of the community as a whole (the democratic approach).

The democratic approach is recommended as the ideal, mainly because of the public participation. But the general public may not want to assume responsibility for deciding priorities (see below).

Total Quality Management

Total Quality Management (TQM) means that every worker in the organisation is encouraged to produce a service that satisfies the customers. There is a lack of consensus about the best way to implement TQM, as evidenced by the pilot centres of the NHS Management Executive's TQM initiative. For example:

- some centres interpreted TQM to include training in 'customer' awareness of all staff; others reserved it for middle and senior management;

- some centres carried out surveys of perceptions of health service; others carried out surveys of satisfaction with them;
- some carried out improvements in the physical environment; others looked at the accessibility for people with disabilities; others looked at transport services for people recovered from an acute illness on discharge from hospital;
- some installed an intercom system;
- some offered patients' information leaflets.

(IPPR Social Policy Paper No. 5 1991)

TQM may give organisations a strong sense of purpose by offering staff at all levels an active role in the pursuit of quality — so it could empower workers at lower levels with a strong sense of commitment. Moreover, its holistic approach should encourage integrated strategies for planning and delivery of services. Whether it does all these things is not clear. In some hospitals the implementation of TQM policy appears to work well. Others are sceptical — although this may be because they have less experience of it.

One thing is certain: TQM cannot be introduced in any useful way without a cost. Organisations have to be prepared to invest in it and allocate resources and time for employees to engage in it. Ultimately, TQM is as good as — and no better than — the sum of the effects of measures invoked in its name. And, as said earlier, the effects of measures in the clinical arena are clinical outcomes — which cannot yet be measured.

Audit

Anxieties about medical audit

The whole issue of responsibility for audit is receiving a great deal of attention because of a recent report (1993) showing that a group of patients at the Royal Orthopaedic Hospital in Birmingham were wrongly diagnosed. Some patients were treated for cancers they did not have; some did not receive treatment they needed. This particular crisis may be debated by public enquiry but there is no doubt that pressure will be exerted to expand supervision of medical practice into the lay arena.

We would question the effectiveness of medical audit, as it stands at present, under the following headings:

Is audit established?

It is very early in the post NHS reform era to expect too much of medical audit. Most hospitals/Trusts are attempting to implement some system which fulfils all the required criteria, but this takes time. In our own Unit it would be impossible to document, via audit, that a clinical colleague was guilty of less than 'ideal' practice.

Who should do it?

In Chapter 4 we said that a fundamental principle of medical audit is that medical work be reviewed by medical peers. Inevitably, the immediate reaction by some parties, after a crisis such as the one in Birmingham, is to accuse doctors of 'closing ranks' and 'covering-up' the mistakes of colleagues. However, in this case at least, this appears not to have been true. The medical staff observing the problem appeared to have had no power to do anything about it.

Guidelines

There are no medical audit guidelines for dealing with issues such as this, and perhaps audit should not be invoked. Medical audit should perhaps only concern itself with problems that can be overcome locally by peer pressure.

Funding and resources

It must not be forgotten that less than ideal clinical practice is not always the fault of the clinician. There may be a lack of resources or staff, clinics may be too large, etc. So audit should be used to identify the reasons for any shortcomings in practice and to ensure that steps are taken to correct them.

Theory of the bad apple

An unfortunate inference of practice scrutiny is that clinicians are not doing a good job; that their medical practice may not be ideal; that bad practice has to be rooted out. If audit is used simply as a fault-finding exercise (the 'theory of the bad apple'), there will undoubtedly be continuing opposition to it. But, in the aftermath of the Birmingham crisis, it will be argued that, had a proper system of medical audit been in place, the anomalous diagnoses would have been spotted.

The sad part about the recent crisis is that there appear to have been definite medical mistakes but no mechanism for highlighting them earlier. Many clinicians will have heard reports of 'less than ideal practice' being followed by colleagues. These reports are almost always based on heresay; there has been no way of proving or disproving them. Should audit do this? If so, it seems unable to do so at present.

The report of the Regional Medical Audit Coordinators Committee and Confederation of Colleges' Audit Working Group (February 1993) envisaged that within the next 5 years audit will have a number of targets, including :

- it will be multidisciplinary and part of hospital wide quality management programmes;
- it will be informed by purchaser/provider/patients. It will also take into account College priorities;
- it will increasingly demonstrate cost effectiveness to provider, purchaser and the public;
- it will increasingly focus on outcomes and their relationships to processes of care.

Increasingly, purchasers have a legitimate interest in ensuring that effective audit is in place in hospitals and community units, and some agreement as to the nature of audit programmes may already be enshrined in the contract. Guidance within the circular (Clinical Audit in HCHS 1993) recommends that Regions should ensure that DPHs have an enhanced role in agreeing audit programmes with provider units, and a mechanism for open discussion should be established between purchasers and providers at least annually to discuss audit progress, programmes and outcomes.

Some £50m has been made available for audit nationally in 1993/94 — forward thinking units will be capitalising on this allocation. However, in our view audit is still poorly resourced and there is a great deal of bureaucracy obstructing the process of gaining audit monies. Even in our own Directorate, which comprises a large number of clinical staff and has a high patient throughput, there is no external provision for general audit assistants.

Rationing

Health Authorities cannot afford to fund all treatments. In fact rationing has existed in some form or another for some time. Patients added to waiting lists, for example, have usually been given a priority value, e.g. urgent, soon, routine, depending on the perceived seriousness of their condition. In some parts of the country there are still long waiting lists (up to 2 years in some areas), so these patients can be said to be discriminated against.

But now the issue of rationing is in open debate. The expansion in medical technology and expertise is exponential. Even if more of the GNP were injected into the NHS, there would never be enough to satisfy all demands. This is not to say that the NHS does not need more resource, but that demand will always exceed supply. So rationing is inevitable and it is likely to be used on an increasing scale.

The dilemma is accepting this fact whilst acknowledging that being seduced into accepting rationing will give politicians the perfect excuse not to increase resources (Hancock 1993). Some may say that the current political hype about rationing marks the thin end of a wedge. More and more services may be taken out of the NHS.

Priority lists

The subject is assuming a high profile because of a number of events. One of these is the Oregon experiment (named after the US state which developed it). In Oregon, instead of rationing health care by queueing, the health authorities have drawn up a list of medical conditions that will be eligible for Medicaid cover. The previous practice was that the very poor were covered by Medicaid but the intermediate population had no access to any state health care. This group comprised a large part of the population. The plan was to extend non-private health care to the entire population, but to limit the treatments available. After a great deal of consultation with the community and with health care professionals, approximately 700 medical treatments were ranked on the basis of a complex formula that considered efficacy, the seriousness of the disease, the prevalence of the disease and the cost. Medical treatments below a certain rank will not be covered. The plan means that the majority of the population do have (some) access to non-private medical care, but that all the population have to pay for some things.

In the UK, the same practice is developing under the guise of '*explicit funding*'. Some Health Authorities are drawing up lists of procedures they are prepared to carry out free of charge and others for which the patient will have to pay. The services 'dropped' tend to be for non-life-threatening conditions, e.g. the list of procedures not available on the NHS published by North Nottingham includes liposuction, repair of breast ptosis, breast augmentation, gender reassignment, removal of tattoos and reversal of sterilisations. Many of us would agree with such a list, because these operations are not usually directly beneficial to health. In general, life-threatening disorders assume high priority: IVF, cosmetic treatments and varicose veins are low on the lists.

Similar rationing programmes are currently being investigated in other parts of the world, in particular New Zealand and the Netherlands. In the Netherlands priorities have been set according to what is necessary, effective and efficient. In vitro fertilisation is excluded because it is not necessary, homeopathy because it is not effective and dental care for adults because it should be an individual rather than a community responsibility.

Of course, this is contrary to the founding principles of the NHS established by Bevan in 1948, so the establishment of priority lists has caused a great deal of controversy and has raised a number of ethical issues. For example, do you penalise smokers if they develop lung cancer and require chest surgery? Interestingly, in Oregon, alcohol dependency is considered to be a disability and therefore people with cirrhosis will not be denied liver transplants.

QALYS and other methods of prioritising

For some time Williams (1985, 1987) has advocated that the Quality-Adjusted-Life-Year (QALY) should be the yardstick for prioritising health care. Based on the notion that if a year of healthy life-expectancy is worth 1, then an unhealthy year is worth less than 1, and the lower the score the worse the quality of life of the patient. Being dead is zero, but there will be some states of illness which carry scores of less than zero. If this system of measurement were to be adopted, some types of disability (the treatment for which might be expensive) would not be discriminated against (but might be under the Oregon rules). But in a recent survey the public and health purchasers put high priority on prevention, namely childhood immunisation. So, which should be the yardstick, life-threatening conditions, quality of life or prevention of disease?

Who should decide?

Whilst the health authorities in Oregon were praised (by President Clinton, no less) for their openness and their involvement of the public in decision making, there appears to be a great deal of unease in the UK about who should make the decisions. Many doctors and health authorities are prepared to 'pass the buck' to the general public, but are patients themselves able to take this responsibility? No one wants to take the lead in identifying those people who are less equal than others. At a recent conference organised by BMJ, BMA, King's Fund and Patients

Association, it was agreed that whilst priority setting was inevitable, no one knew how it should be done or who should do it.

The Health of the Nation White Paper targets key areas for improving the nation's health, but apart from this initiative there are no clear guidelines on how Health Authorities should prioritise care.

Information/clinical outcomes

Parliamentary jargon does not help.

"This process [rationing] should be led by purchasers and they should base their decisions on national priorities, public consultation and research based evidence supported by professional advice" ....and "understanding the effectiveness of clinical interventions is the key to proper priority setting"

(Secretary of State for Health 1993)

Whilst there is consensus that priority decisions should be based on clinical outcomes, these are not measurable at present. In a study of six Health Authorities lack of information on the effectiveness of health care interventions as a guide to priority setting was seen as a major problem (Ham 1993). The legacy that you have inherited as a doctor–manager is that there are no scientific data on which to base these decisions. The cost effectiveness of most interventions is not measured.

The Hospital Inpatient Enquiry (HIPE) was discontinued in 1985/86 and was replaced by Korner, which has still not produced reliable data in such crucial a field as inpatient mortality. Purchasers and providers still have no information to distinguish between walking alive and dead discharges. It is still impossible to answer simple questions such as who is doing what surgery in which hospital and with what success. So how can anyone allocate or ration care amongst competing patients when faced with this level of ignorance?

However, there is an argument in favour of rationing. Maynard (1993) makes a valid comment: although it is difficult to ration in ignorance, only when you begin to ration will you create the incentive to measure scientifically and to determine the cost effectiveness of unproven therapies.

Medical staffing levels

Some of the prevalent issues relating to medical staffing have been referred to briefly in Chapter 5. The intention in that chapter was to discuss manpower planning in a general management sense. However, there are national changes occurring in medical manpower which you, as doctor–manager, must understand in some detail because the sequelae of these changes will have considerable impact on your department's functions. The issues include 'Achieving a Balance', Safety Net; junior doctors: the New Deal; and consultant expansion.

The New Deal: hours of duty

As of April 1st 1993, the maximum average contracted hours of duty for doctors in training should not exceed 83 per week. The next target is the reduction of average contracted hours of duty to a maximum of 72 (by December 1994). Many doctors believe that this target cannot be achieved other than by the implementation of some sort of shift system (Doyle 1991). The arguments for and against shift systems are presented frequently in the medical press. Apart from lack of continuity of patient care, there are ramifications with regard to teaching, teamwork and firm allegience.

Now the April 1993 deadline has passed, there has been some relaxation of effort in deciding how to implement the next change because it is some time off. But a 72-hour working week for all junior staff will have immense consequences: even if full shift systems are not required, there will have to be a major change in the working patterns of all medical staff. As doctor–manager you will have to implement this change.

There is anxiety amongst many senior doctors about who will do the work. You need to start making plans now to cope with this problem, otherwise it will overtake you (proactive *vs* reactive management).

Achieving a Balance

The basic principles whereby career aspirations can be fulfilled are supported both by doctors and Health Authorities. However, reducing or limiting the quotas for registrars in line with potential consultant vacancies, inevitably imposes greater strain on the consultant grade.

Consultant expansion

The Government is allocating £7.3m for 125 new consultant posts to ease this process. These will be in addition to the 350 consultant posts and 150 staff-grade posts already being established from allocations totalling £24.5m. But this number of new consultants is inadequate and will probably be insufficient to cover the deficit. There needs to be a doubling of consultant posts to do the work.

Downie (1993) asks whether the objectives of the New Deal can be achieved. He admits that by August 1992 only 6.4% of training posts in the English Regions were in shift systems. Furthermore, whilst 1993 targets might have been met, authorities are less hopeful about the 1994 72-hour deadline.

Training

Training is under scrutiny and will be more carefully supervised in future with Regional Postgraduate Deans exercising control over Regional funds identified for all junior doctors' training. As of 1st April 1993, Postgraduate Deans control 50% of the training grade budget and they would like it all. Teaching services are now commissioned from Trust hospitals which compete with each other to win contracts to teach junior doctors.

Together with the restructuring of hospital services in the wake of the NHS reforms, the internal market developing in the teaching arena means that you, as doctor–manager, have competition on all sides. The Regional Deans may develop mechanisms for withdrawing funds from posts that provide inadequate training, so you may lose medical jobs, and your Chief Executive will threaten you with non-medical job losses if contracts are lost.

The NHS Management Executive suggested that purchasers should recognise the training element in hospital practice and include an educational contract element in their specifications. If this happens, it will mean that purchasers are really interested in quality.

Career structure

The career structure of hospital doctors will also undergo a major reorganisation. A shortfall of doctors needed to cover all the NHS services is likely in the next 10–20 years (DoH 1992a), but how this can be solved is not yet clear. The implementation of flexible working hours is really only applicable to women doctors with family commitments.

Apart from this, more doctors are needed if we are to conform to EC rules, the New Deal, etc. It is likely that the Government will continue to increase the number of consultant posts, but this increase will have to be substantial. Some new posts may have to be provided within present budgets by switching resources from other areas where they are not needed. But new consultant posts, which are being sold as a real input into the NHS, really do not help the service unless there are backup and support staff to go with them.

Another way of increasing the number of medical staff is by raising the number of staff doctors. It has been proposed that they be raised from 10% to 12.5% of the total number of consultants. This has generated anxiety amongst some doctors because Trusts do not have to keep to national terms and conditions of service, so their contracts may be different from the norm. Furthermore, staff grade doctors are less expensive than consultants, so they are a cheaper way of providing the service.

Much more important is the Calman report on specialist medical training. The working party, chaired by the Chief Medical Officer, has recommended that the length of specialist training in this country be substantially reduced to fall in line with the EC. This will increase markedly the number of doctors eligible to become consultants — and they will become consultants for the reasons described, i.e. the reduction in junior doctors' hours; the potential reduction in numbers of junior staff secondary to training requirement standards; and the projected shortfall in doctors over the next decade.

Will patient care be compromised? It is the view of one of us (JRS) that the level of experience of specialists entering consultant practice in the UK is already being eroded by shorter hours and lack of supervision. We seem already to be producing consultants who might not be able to handle certain emergencies or certain types of medical problem. This will be exacerbated if doctors become independent specialists much earlier in their careers than at present. There is no answer to this: we have to fall in line with EC practice where experience (in our view) is less clinical and much narrower.

Summary

Whilst the intention of this chapter was to be a critical commentary, we made it clear at the start that we have been greatly excited by working in the new system. The NHS reforms have brought many benefits. It has been stressed that we are still at an early stage of implementing them, and some of the anxieties may be unfounded. However, this means also the reforms have not yet had time to bite. There may still be more turbulent times ahead. The doctor–manager must be aware of this and maintain a critical (although constructive) approach to any change.

Attention was drawn earlier in the chapter to some of the disadvantages arising from GP fundholding and the internal market. This might become a minor irritation when Health Authorities become more sophisticated in the use of *their* purchasing power — which amounts to much more than that of GP fundholders (say, £300m compared to £2m).

As far as the internal market is concerned, healthy competition is to be welcomed, but there is some evidence from the NHS and industry that too much competition is unhealthy. The commercial world is being encouraged to go for *partnership sourcing* — a strategy that the CBI is promoting. Industrial and commercial organisations are being urged to work together and avoid short-term contracts and destructive competition. To quote Clive Bone:

"The old system, which was based on a mindless search for the lowest price...... has comprehensively been proved to be the wrong way of doing things..... If you want quality and value for money in healthcare then follow the partnership principle. This means that fundholders and purchasers must take a long-term view and work with service suppliers with a sense of common purpose to attain the standards of service they want to achieve".

(Bone 1993)

In the NHS there is undoubtedly less collaboration between hospital units now than before the internal market (e.g. in research projects). Also, some small and specialist medical services (e.g. laboratories providing rare assay services) may find themselves without resource (Lancet 1993).

The seeming shortfall of resource in many areas inside the hospital unit is harder to accept when we are told that, on average, one-third of the money allocated thus far to GP fundholders has been, or is being, used to develop practice premises.

Some GP fundholders, in their search for a better deal for patients still cause much anxiety. The provision, by hospital consultants, of GP or 'in house' clinics, for example, is a splendid service for a small group of patients, but is not cost-effective for the whole population.

On top of this, hospital doctors are increasingly frustrated by not having direct access to the contracting process. Currently, there is no formal framework for them to be an integral part of the contracting for services. However, these are early days, and most purchasers acknowledge the need for greater collaboration with service clinicians.

There are some GPs who believe a coordinated group of non-fundholders may be in a better position objectively to view purchaser and provider data (Eve & Hodgkin 1991). Quality of service as perceived by patients and GPs would, in their view, be better assessed if they were independent of both purchaser and provider, reducing the conflicts of interest of purchasers (more care *vs* better care) and the likelihood of cartels among providers. However, the move now is towards the collaboration of GP, patients and purchaser. Clearly, we have to move towards a system of closer collaboration between purchasers and providers, with less emphasis on competition and more on the overall benefit to the population of patients.

Finally, although collaboration in other areas of the service may yet be far from ideal, we must draw attention to the satisfaction of a doctor–manager working in close association with a Business Manager for the benefit of a Directorate as a whole.

Further reading

Abel-Smith B
1993 Challenges to come for the NHS. Hospital Update Plus February

Bone C
1993 Association for Quality in Health Care Seminar. Quoted by Kirby

Bull A R
1993 Difficult choices in health care. Journal of Management in Medicine 7: 64–67

Coulter A
1992 Fundholding general practices. British Medical Journal 304: 397–398

Day P, Klein R
1991 Variations in budgets of fundholding practices. British Medical Journal 303: 168–170

Department of Health and Social Security
1986 Hospital Medical Staffing: Achieving a Balance. DHSS, London

Department of Health and Social Security
1987 Hospital Medical Staffing: Achieving a Balance- plan for action. DHSS, London

Department of Health
1991 Junior Doctors: The New Deal. Hours of work of doctors in training: working arrangements for doctors and dentists in training. NHSME, London

Department of Health
1992a Funding of hospital medical and dental training grade posts. NHSME, London

Department of Health
1992b Planning the Medical Workforce. Medical manpower standing advisory committee: first report, Department of Health, London

Department of Health
1993a Hospital Doctors: Training for the Future. A consultative document from the working group on specialist medical training (The Calman Report)

Department of Health
1993b NHSME Circular EL (93) 34. Audit and the Purchaser/Provider Interaction. NHSME, London

Downie R
1993 The New Deal: can we do it? British Journal of Hospital Medicine 49: 607–609

Doyle P
1991 Junior doctors: The New Deal. Changing patterns of work. British Medical Journal 303: 982–984

Editorial
1993a Medical training goes to market. Hospital Doctor May: 11

Editorial
1993b Future of small and

specialised medical services in Britain. Lancet 342: 316

Eve R, Hodgkin P
1991 In praise of non-fundholding practices. British Medical Journal 303: 167–168

Ham C
1993 Priority setting in the NHS: reports from six districts. British Medical Journal 307: 435–438

Hancock C
1993 Debate on priorities convened by BMJ, BMA, King's Fund and Patients Association. British Medical Journal 306: 737

Kirby J
1993 Where Quality Care is Marked. Health Care Management January: 20–22

Kitzhaber J A
1993 Prioritising health services in an era of limits: the Oregon experience. British Medical Journal 307: 373–377

Klein R
1993 Dimensions of rationing: who should do what? British Medical Journal 307: 309–311

Maynard A
1993 Never mind the cost-savings, will it win votes? Health Care Management March: 50–51

Pfeffer N, Coote A
1991 Is Quality Good for You? The Institute for Public Policy Research, Social Policy Paper No. 5

Roland M
1991 Fundholding and cash limits in primary care: blight or blessing? British Medical Journal 303: 171–172

Secretary of State for Health
1991 The Health of the Nation: a consultative document for health in England. HMSO, London

Secretary of State for Health
1993 Debate on priorities. Joint meeting of BMJ, BMA, King's Fund and Patients Association. British Medical Journal. 306: 737. Quoted in Health Care Management February: 23

Weiner J, Ferriss D
1990 GP budget holding in the UK: lessons from America. King's Fund Institute, London

Williams A
1985 The value of QALYS. Health and Social Services Journal, July: 3–5

Williams A
1987 How should NHS priorities be determined? Hospital Update April: 261–263, 341

Index